DEMOCRACY DENIED

DEMOCRACY DENIED:
Five Lectures on U.S. Politics

Victor Wallis

Introduction by
Johanna Fernández

Illustrations by
Kevin "Rashid" Johnson

AFRICA WORLD PRESS
TRENTON | LONDON | CAPE TOWN | NAIROBI | ADDIS ABABA | ASMARA | IBADAN | NEW DELHI

AFRICA WORLD PRESS
541 West Ingham Avenue | Suite B
Trenton, New Jersey 08638

Copyright © 2019 Victor Wallis

All rights reserved. No part of this publication may be reproduced, stored in a retrieval system or transmitted in any form or by any means electronic, mechanical, photocopying, recording or otherwise without the prior written permission of the publisher.

Book design: Lemlem Tadesse
Cover design: Ashraful Haque

Cataloging-in-Publication Data may be obtained from the Library of Congress.

ISBNs: 978-1-56902-614-4 (HB)
       978-1-56902-615-1 (PB)

DEDICATION

To students of all ages and every condition
who seek to understand the world in order to change it

TABLE OF CONTENTS

Preface ix

Introduction xv
Johanna Fernández

American "Exceptionalism": US Institutions in
Comparative Perspective 1

US Imperialism: From Continental Expansion to
Global Intervention 21

From Slavery to Mass Incarceration: The Saga of
African-Descended People in the United States 47

Can the Left Become a Major Player in US Politics? .. 69

The Current US Political Scene 91

Index 115

PREFACE

This book originated as an attempt to explain US politics to a non-US audience. The audience happened to be Chinese, but the particular setting of my lectures had no bearing on the content of what I said. My arguments would have been the same for any non-US audience and, as I quickly realized, also the same – apart from my insertion of a few extra background details – for an audience within the United States.

The one consequence of the English/Chinese language-barrier was that I had to write out the complete texts in advance, for the translators. That initially unwelcome requirement – which I learned of only at the last minute – transformed what would otherwise have been a set of merely informal reflections into a complete draft of this book.

I am grateful to Professor Zhao Yulan and to the Institute of Marxism at Renmin University of China (RUC) for inviting me to lecture there, and to the Institute's graduate students and junior faculty for making possible, through their translations of my remarks, a productive conversation.

Inez Hedges was my companion on this trip, as on many others since our joint-teaching semester 30+ years ago. She enriched my experience of China, partly by her own engagement with the country's language and culture. We were welcomed and made to feel at home not only by our faculty colleagues but also by the students we met, most especially by Kang Jiaxin and Wang Sai.

The lectures were presented in May/June 2018; events and references have been updated here through late 2018. The invitation to speak at RUC came after a May 2016 visit to several Chinese institutions, in which I was part of a small international delegation organized by my friend and editorial colleague (at *Socialism and Democracy*), Marcello Musto.

Professor Zhao, in inviting me to RUC, left it up to me to propose the lecture topics. I saw this as an opportunity to put together my thoughts on subjects that many authors have addressed in greater depth, but on which I would now be able to offer the kind of wide-ranging yet concise overview that the routines of course-work, editing, and activism rarely leave time for.

My lectures took place prior to the clashes that began last July at several Chinese universities (including RUC), in which Marxist students were expelled for supporting labor organizers.[1] From what I know, I support the

---

1 https://chinadigitaltimes.net/2018/11/students-assaulted-amid-crackdown-on-marxist-activism/

students and deplore the reprisals taken against them. But China's official Marxism has contradictory effects. Although it is invoked in support of arbitrary measures, it nonetheless provides, albeit indirectly, an opening for critical reflections on class power.[2] Radical students may draw from this, and outsiders may contribute to it, even if their focus is on other countries.

The only part of these lectures that was aimed specifically at my Chinese listeners was a few paragraphs at the very beginning – omitted here – where I cautioned them against the inclination, popular among many Chinese students, to take dominant US practice in matters of economics and politics as some kind of model that they should seek to emulate.

After my return from China, I circulated the lecture-texts to a number of friends, including especially individuals caught up in the bowels of the outsized US prison system. Politically aware prisoners are among the most eager students I know, and their responses encouraged me to make the texts more widely available. The collective experience of these prisoners had already informed much of what I sought to communicate; I hope they will find in my words a recognition of the importance of their struggles.

Among my incarcerated readers, Kevin "Rashid" Johnson has been much more than a student. He plays a

---

2 See Robert Ware, "Reflections on Chinese Marxism," *Socialism and Democracy* 27:1 (March 2013).

leading role in the movement to transform the institutions that are the subject of this book. He is not only a revolutionary organizer, but also a reporter (exposing prison abuse), a theoretician (the author of two books) and, as well, an extraordinary political artist. His drawings strikingly dramatize the arguments of this text. I am grateful to him for his willingness to let me include them.

It has been a pleasure to work with Kassahun Checole and his team at Africa World Press. I thank my friend and colleague Teodros Kiros for introducing me to Kassahun. It was Kassahun who suggested that this book might be enhanced not only by illustrations but also by a guest-introduction.

For this latter task, no one is more suited than Johanna Fernández, both as a scholar of US history and as a dedicated and inspiring activist, most prominently, in the campaign to free Mumia Abu-Jamal – the imprisoned journalist whose saga epitomizes the denial of democracy in this country. I am honored by her generous collaboration. Before writing the Introduction, she gave my text a close reading and made numerous suggestions that significantly strengthened its argument. For all this, I am most grateful to her.

We all live this period under the cloud of economic austerity and ecological collapse – with the attendant extremes of mass discontent (if not unbearable suffering), increasingly aggressive power plays, and growing displacement of peoples. This gives added urgency to the task of creating a sounder social order. As you read this book, I hope you will find in its narrative some of the insights you will need, if you're in the US, in order to carry this task forward, and, if you are elsewhere in the world, to understand the enormity of the challenge that we are up against.

Victor Wallis
Somerville, Massachusetts
January 2019

INTRODUCTION
Johanna Fernández

> History, as nearly no one seems to know, is not merely something to be read. And it does not refer merely, or even principally, to the past. On the contrary, the great force of history comes from the fact that we carry it within us, are unconsciously controlled by it in many ways, and history is literally present in all that we do. It could scarcely be otherwise, since it is to history that we owe our frames of reference, our identities, and our aspirations.
>
> —James Baldwin, 1965

To those looking in from the outside, America during the second decade of the 21st century began to look like an open-ward, 19th-century madhouse—absurdity and violent cruelty included.

It wasn't always this way. Or was it?

This compendium walks us through the defining features and problems of American society. Author Victor Wallis initially delivered these lectures to Chinese scholars and graduate students in their homeland. Writing for such an audience demanded an exacting selection and analysis of the major themes and problems in American society. The politics needed to be accessible to a broad audience.

Wallis met the challenge. A long-standing senior editor of the journal *Socialism and Democracy*, he is uniquely positioned to curate a fresh digest of American history. In *Democracy Denied*, he seamlessly connects America's past and present, and employs a class analysis of history to illuminate the forces driving the country's trajectory and its underbelly. As a long-time activist on behalf of prisoners' rights (having spent hundreds of hours since the 1970s corresponding with prisoners across the country), he has also secured the artwork of Kevin "Rashid" Johnson for this volume. Johnson is a prisoner and self-proclaimed black revolutionary with a dramatic history of transformation from drug dealer to radical jailhouse organizer, prolific writer and artist.[1] His drawings are haunting and meticulously complex. They bring to life and humanize the themes of these lectures.

In the waning days of the 20th century, the U.S. was still the imagined global almshouse to the persecuted and the poor. But it quickly turned into a place where thousands of armed white supremacists, no longer cloaked in hoods, marched in the public square, emboldened by an openly racist president hell-bent on building a border wall to keep out "the Mexicans." An anomaly on the world stage, America has had more mass shootings than any other country. But in the 21st century, that once-infrequent phenomenon became an everyday

---

1 See *Defying the Tomb: Selected Prison Writings and Art of Kevin "Rashid" Johnson* (Montreal: Kersplebedeb, 2010).

feature in churches and schools across the nation—carried out, in the main, by deranged white gunmen. America also became the place where in 2018 a presidential decree mandated separating children from their migrant mothers as a deterrent to those en route to the U.S. southern border after fleeing their countries' political and economic crises. America also became the country whose commander in chief bragged about dropping "the mother of all bombs" on an already militarily disfigured Afghanistan and ordered the destruction of all Environmental Protection Agency studies and the firing of all its scientists. Unrecognizable to many, America became the country where, amidst a public debate about rape in 2016, half of the electorate voted for and elected a presidential candidate who explained to the media that he subdues women by "grabbing them by the pussy."

These social currents may seem aberrant, but as Victor Wallis tells us in these pages, they have antecedents in North America's early history. The extreme character of contemporary problems in the U.S., however, lay in the history of its recent past. The alarming right-wing surge in American society in the second decade of the 21st century represents the consolidation and triumph of the backlash to the social movements of the Sixties and the defeat of the U.S. in the Vietnam War, which also included the repression and defeat of the sixties Left. This compact collection of five edited lectures answers the question of why.

Wallis draws on new studies that show the continuum between early colonial history and the American Revolution. The 18th-century settler colonial project that became the United States rested on the violent appropriation of land from the native people of North America and control of enslaved African labor. In self-defense, the indigenous population responded with an early form of guerrilla war; Africans either escaped or organized slave rebellions. In this contest, European elites responded with "savage war" dependent on the dehumanization of those whose lands and freedom they usurped. They also weaponized the homes of Europeans of all classes. As scholar of Native American history Roxanne Dunbar-Ortiz recounts, "In 1658, the colony ordered every settler home to have a functioning firearm; subsidized those who couldn't afford them; and fined homes without functioning weapons and individuals who traveled to public meetings without them. In time this became the basis of forced militia and slave patrol inscription among white men of all classes."[2]

In other words, racialized violence, white supremacy, and the culture of military-grade gun love are not passing fads in America. This ghastly triumvirate was present at

---

[2] Roxanne Dunbar-Ortiz, *Loaded: A Disarming History of the Second Amendment* (San Francisco: City Lights Books, 2018), 35. See also Gerald Horne, *The Counter-Revolution of 1776: Slave Resistance and the Origins of the United States of America* (New York: NYU Press, 2014).

the creation in our country. Without its normalization, the nascent state would not have secured, maintained, and extended its emerging borders.

Deftly organized and assembled, this primer examines the nation through five major thematic frames: American exceptionalism, U.S. imperialism, race in America, the contours of the U.S. Left, and contemporary American politics. Together they distill the defining features of American society—-its political institutions, myths and cultural practices, distinctive brand of unrestrained capitalism, and its socialist tradition and the challenges to it.

Wallis presents his analytical framework at the outset. He underscores the social relations of production of the United States' first major labor system, the conditions under which it emerged and its long-term social consequences. He observes that a substantial region of the country's original colonial-settler project developed "a plantation economy based on slave labor." The racial antagonism that slavery produced, he argues, created a deep divide within the American working class that has rendered it the most politically weak in the advanced capitalist world.

The tenacity of racism in American history reflects its centrality to America's origin story *and* to its development as a modern, industrial capitalist economy. In the early 19th century the global sales of cotton produced by American slaves made up 50% of U.S. exports. Domestically, the industrial revolution in the

North was made possible because of its proximity to the South's Cotton Kingdom whose vast production, holdings and wealth also fueled the rapid development and maturation of American capitalism's key industries: investment banking, real estate, and insurance. On the eve of the American Civil War, the American South's four million African slaves had enriched the southern plantocracy mightily. Together with that of their forebears, their collective labor produced the second wealthiest society humanity had seen up to that date, second only to the British Empire.[3]

As Barbara Fields demonstrates in her essay, "Slavery, Race and Ideology in the United States," race ideology emerged to rationalize slavery over time, because of "the incorporation of Africans and their descendants into a polity and society in which they lacked rights that others not only took for granted, but claimed as a matter of self-evident natural law."[4] Given the dominance of racism in the U.S. and beyond, it bears repeating that scientists long ago determined that the traits associated with race—skin color, facial features,

---

3 Sven Beckert, Laird Bell, and Seth Rockman, *Slavery's Capitalism: A New History of American Economic Development* (Philadelphia: University of Pennsylvania Press, 2016); Edward Baptiste, *Half Has Never Been Told: Slavery and the Making of American Capitalism* (New Yok: Basic Books, 2016).

4 Barbara Jeanne Fields, "Slavery, Race, and Ideology in the United States of America," *New Left Review*, 1st Series, no. 181 (May-June 1990), 106.

and hair texture—are genetically superficial traits signaling human diversity, which have little biological meaning. In short, the meanings humans attribute to race, about intelligence and capacity, are produced by society; they are not biologically determined.[5] But logic and proof are no match for race ideology, especially in the U.S. where its assumptions are as ingrained as the institution of slavery, which persists in its prisons as allowed in a clause of the 13th Amendment, the Civil War era measure that ended plantation slavery.

Fought, in part, over the question of slavery's expansion into the continent's Western territory, the Civil War cleared the way for the rapid development of American industrial capitalism.[6] These pages are attentive to American capitalism's most enduring myths, among them the belief in individual rather than collective advancement. By the end of the 19th century, as the country became one of the world's major producers of industrial goods, government advisers began to stress the importance of naval power. American capitalism's drive for new markets inevitably led to imperial pursuits and war.

---

5 Robert W. Sussman, *The Myth of Race: The Troubling Persistence of an Unscientific Idea* (Cambridge: Harvard University Press, 2014); Stephen Jay Gould, *The Mismeasure of Man* (New York: W.W. Norton & Co., 1981).

6 William Rosen, *The Most Powerful Idea in the World: A Story of Steam, Industry and Invention* (Chicago: University of Chicago Press, 2012).

At a moment when American imperialism continues its path of destruction across the world, these pages skillfully zero in on the most defining features of American expansion, which has historically managed to rationalize its genocidal military operations with a rhetoric of righteous commitment to democracy. Fresh and lucid, Wallis's analyses unveil an underlying unity of imperial and domestic policies, for example, that both rely on racialized dehumanization of the enemy. The U.S. practice of savage war against Native Americans and against the people of Japan, Korea and Vietnam finds a domestic corollary in capital punishment. Wallis, who has written extensively on the environment, reminds us that the consequences of empire and war are more alarming "as earth's eco-structure collapses into fire and flood."[7]

Among the lessons to take away from *Democracy Denied* is the necessity for political organizing separate from the Democratic Party. In the mid-20th century the Democratic Party began to position itself as the representative of working people, the poor and oppressed sectors of the country within the two-party system. However, while Democratic politicians have absorbed the rhetoric of social movements, their party

---

[7] Below, 23; see also Victor Wallis, *Red-Green Revolution: The Politics and Technology of Ecosocialism* (Toronto and Chicago: Political Animal Press, 2018).

has always represented and advanced the interests of American capitalism and empire.

In fact, they have arguably been able to advance regressive platforms that would have produced broader resistance had they been passed by their overtly conservative counterparts, the Republicans. For example, the extreme right-wing political current that gathered steam and groped for organizational form in 21st-century America did not emerge out of nowhere. Much of its ideology was institutionalized and amplified during the 1990s though the bipartisanship of Democratic President Bill Clinton. Clinton was perhaps the most sophisticated advocate of harsh anti-crime, anti-welfare, anti-immigrant, and anti-terrorism legislation. In the face of widespread economic anxiety among Americans due to a long-term pattern of deindustrialization, declining wages and the elimination of healthcare benefits, politicians eagerly advanced legislation that blamed black people, poor women, immigrants and Muslims for the country's ills.

The real problem, however, was neoliberalism— a strategy employed by captains of American capitalism to overcome the declining rate of profit in American industry.[8] While public policy focused on scapegoats, and politicians blamed the movements of the Sixties for their supposed excesses, poor, working- and middle-

---

8   On Neoliberalism see David Harvey, *A Brief History of Neoliberalism* (Oxford: Oxford University Press, 2007).

class white people in the U.S. remained confused about the source of their discontent.

Beginning in the early 1970s, American goods were out-priced in the world market by those produced and sold by Japan and Germany, whose economies were up and running again after having been rebuilt in the postwar years with the latest technology.[9] In response, American business partnered with the U.S. government to rescue its capital with a program of draconian wage cuts, the elimination of benefits like healthcare, and union busting.[10] The strategy also included overseas expansion in Latin America and Asia (through policies such as the North American Free Trade Agreement), Wall Street speculation, and widespread de-regulation of industry. By the beginning of the 21st century, working-class white communities across the United States began to reel from deindustrialization and social isolation, conditions that Black Americans and Latinos began to experience decades earlier. The possibility of a class-based offensive, however, remained elusive, but necessary.

Such a project requires re-imagining the American working class, and the rebuilding of an independent Left

---

9 Gérard Duménil and Dominique Lévy, *Capital Resurgent: Roots of the Neoliberal Revolution* (Cambridge: Harvard University Press, 2004), Chapter 3, and Robert Brenner, *The Boom and the Bubble* (New York: Verso Press, 2002), Chapter 1.

10 Mike Davis, *Prisoners of the American Dream* (New York: Verso, 1986), Chapters 4 & 5.

no longer isolated from workers and their communities. The project must simultaneously prioritize, support and strengthen the gathering pace of movements in defense of immigrants and women and against police violence, gender violence, and hetero-normativity.

Regardless of where you reside, *Democracy Denied* can help a new generation of people of conscience learn the contours of power and politics in America. It is also hard medicine and necessary reckoning for *all* Americans. After all, whose community doesn't stand on the precipice of social decay and economic crisis as the world reels from the effects wrought by U.S. empire?

Lecture 1

AMERICAN "EXCEPTIONALISM": US INSTITUTIONS IN COMPARATIVE PERSPECTIVE

On US Institutions

Underlying all other possible observations about the United States is the fact that its colonial-settler origins included the subjection of a substantial region of the country to a plantation economy based on slave labor. We shall look further, in lecture 3, at the particular status and experience of the enslaved population and its descendants, but for the moment we need to examine slavery's impact on the society as a whole: Of all the "advanced" countries, the US is the one whose working class, rent at its core by the "racial" division, has been politically the weakest. The fragmentation arising from this central "racial" chasm within the working class would later be magnified by the arrival of successive waves of immigrants from every corner of the Earth.

Although there was a big surge in unionization during the depression years of the 1930s, the labor movement's top leadership, lacking a class-wide orientation and wedded to the culture of individual advancement ("the American dream"), remained staunchly pro-capitalist and never sought to channel working-class activism in the direction of building an independent political force. As a result, the labor movement, despite the combativeness it displayed in its earlier years, succumbed easily after 1945 to anticommunist legislation, which led to the expulsion from its ranks of many of its most dedicated organizers.

Moreover, the "business unionism" model that predominated already in the 1930s–the individualistic alternative to class conscious or "social-movement" unionism[1]–has meant that labor unions competed against one another as service-providers and, with few exceptions, failed to demand the creation of *government* services of the kind that are taken for granted in other advanced capitalist countries, such as adequate public transportation and universal healthcare.[2] The leadership of the labor movement remained reflexively loyal to the

---

[1] See Kim Moody, *Workers in a Lean World: Unions in the International Economy* (London: Verso, 1997).

[2] The ill-conceived idea of tying health insurance to one's job is a uniquely US phenomenon. On its trade-union origins, see Marie Gottschalk, *The Shadow Welfare State: Labor, Business, and the Politics of Healthcare in the United States* (Ithaca, NY: ILR Press, 2000).

Democratic party, despite the latter's subservience to corporate interests. Over the years since the 1950s, union membership has steadily shrunk (amounting now to less than 10% of the labor force), and legislation hostile to labor organizing has been enacted in a majority of US states (in the form of laws – deceptively called "right to work" – that prevent unions from requiring all the workers they represent to pay membership dues).

This whole assault on working-class interests is of course standard capitalist practice, but its greater impact in the US reflects a long history marked by unrestrained conquest, encompassing both the epic violence of "Indian removal" and the nightmarish rounding up and enslavement of Africans. These twin scourges gave rise to a corresponding culture whose effects are felt in every dimension of US politics. In this culture we find a complex blend of partly antagonistic stances: on the one hand, an unapologetic claim of entitlement to domination, often rationalized in terms of some kind of "mission"; on the other, a posture of denial, expressed in the form of an assumed commitment to democratic values. To be sure, the country also has an authentic democratic tradition, grounded in popular struggles against oppression.[3] But when the ruling class invokes democracy, it's in order to legitimize its own anti-popular policies.

---

3 See Howard Zinn, *A People's History of the United States* (New York: HarperCollins, 2003).

An early expression of this ideological ruse was the myth of the US as a "young" country, set off against "old" Europe (obviously disregarding the presence in North America of indigenous communities that pre-existed the European arrivals). US institutions, though, despite any initial differences from Europe, were derived from European models. The claim to be a young country is ironic, considering that the US constitution is now the oldest written constitution in the world. The US interestingly distinguishes itself in other ways that defy worldwide modern practice, such as not using the metric system except in scientific writing and not using the 24-hour clock for announcing public events such as travel-schedules. These divergences, although not of great significance in themselves, are nonetheless suggestive of a political culture that, in addition to being anti-democratic internally, tends to scorn international consensus – for example, on the urgency of combating climate change, on outlawing landmines and cluster bombs, on recognizing the rights of women and of children, on prosecuting war crimes (the US has signed only 5 of the United Nations' 18 major Human Rights treaties), on opposing the global marketing of corporate-manufactured "infant formula,"[4] and on not stigmatizing Cuba for its 1959 revolution or the Palestinians for resisting Israeli colonization.

---

4 David Swanson, *Curing Exceptionalism* (Charlottesville, VA: self-published, 2018), 85; *New York Times*, July 9, 2018.

What was touted as "new" at the time of the Republic's founding was the rejection of monarchy. This is typically presented (e.g., in school history textbooks) as reflecting a democratic impulse. In fact, though, the sponsorship of American independence was far from being entirely democratic. This has become increasingly clear in the light of recent historical research.[5]

It has always been apparent that the office of the US presidency has monarchical attributes, in that, unlike the prime minister in a parliamentary system, the president attains office independently of the legislative body. The president thus, in addition to being the country's political leader, took on the ceremonial role of "head of state" which had previously been exercised by kings or queens. But it has long been thought that in the early years of American independence (after 1776 but before the creation of the federal constitution with its strong president), a more popular system of power was evolving.

What has been underscored in recent studies, however, is that the conservative foundations of the US governmental system were not just established in the Constitution, but were also already clearly signaled in the Declaration of Independence. Although the war for independence fought by Britain's 13 North American

---

5 See Gerald Horne, *The Counter-Revolution of 1776: Slave Resistance and the Origins of the United States of America* (New York: NYU Press, 2014).

colonies always included an element of democratic appeal and of popular activism (embodied in the slogan "All men are created equal"), more recognition is now being accorded to other aspects of the Declaration's list of complaints against the British monarchy, namely, concern on the part of American property-owners that the British government intended to outlaw slavery and to restrict settlers from expanding into inland territories inhabited by Indian nations – or what the Declaration of Independence called "merciless Indian savages."

The authors of the US Constitution were quite explicit about their fear of democracy. They expressed this fear in the *Federalist Papers* (articles published in 1788 that presented the Constitution to the general public), especially *Federalist Paper* #10. Here they referred to the benefit of having a large and diverse republic, in which the array of contentious issues would keep the popular majority from becoming aware of its common interest in challenging the power of the large-property owners. Elsewhere in those same *Papers*, the authors noted the various institutional barriers – some of the famous "checks and balances" – that would offset the potential power of the directly elected House of Representatives.[6]

The federal structure of the government was a further factor impeding democratic accountability. As is well known, the separate states served as units within which existing patterns of racial hierarchy – and, later on,

---

6 See Zinn, *A People's History.*

retrograde practices regarding, for example, the influence of religion on social policy and on the study of science in public schools – could be protected against any nationwide demand for progressive change. The fact that every state, regardless of its population, would have two Senators meant that there was systematic underrepresentation of heavily populated zones. Moreover, the very fact that presidential elections are decided on a state-by-state basis (rather than by nationwide vote-totals) means that victory can easily go– as it did in the elections of 2000 and 2016–to a candidate who does not have the greatest overall number of votes.

Although not all the states had slavery at the time of the Constitution, the document was explicitly designed to provide guarantees to slaveholders. Not only was the slave population to be counted (three-fifths of it) for purposes of representation – thus increasing the Southern states' voting power in Congress – even though the slaves had no rights; in addition, the sole non-amendable provision of the Constitution was a guarantee of the continued enforcement of slavery for a definite period after the Constitution went into effect.

Despite certain progressive amendments made to the Constitution since its adoption in 1789, *there has never been a constitutional guarantee of the right to vote*. All amendments extending the right to vote have taken the form of removing previous restrictions; there has never been a proactive statement of inclusiveness. Thus, new legal pretexts for exclusion remained constitutionally permissible. Regulation of voting procedures remains in the hands of the separate states, which can devise various stratagems to make it difficult if not impossible for dissident parties to be officially recognized and also for poor people to vote.

States typically set barriers to impede parties other than the two dominant ones from being included on the ballot. These barriers can be raised or lowered at will. Even if only a small number of states sets the barriers very high (e.g., requiring a very high number of signatures to be collected in a very short period of time in order for a party to be listed), this can block a dissident party from becoming a nationwide contender.

Of particular interest in reference to recent elections, however, have been the obstacles placed in the way of the electoral participation of poor people, especially racial or national minorities. These include: 1) excessive and burdensome identification requirements; 2) restrictions on times available for voting; 3) too few polling places in targeted districts; 4) circulating false and sometimes legally intimidating information suggesting to individuals that they may be disqualified from voting (e.g., because of an unpaid parking ticket); and 5) removal of voters' names from the registry on the invented pretext (based on similarities of names) that they are simultaneously registered in more than one state (an accusation that has never been followed up by an actual prosecution).[7] Outcomes of legislative elections may be further distorted by the manipulation of district-boundaries ("gerrymandering"), so that support for progressive candidates is highly concentrated while support for more conservative candidates is more spread out, making it possible for a party with fewer votes to have a larger number of elected representatives.

More generally, the division of powers between the federal government on the one hand and the separate states on the other has, throughout the country's history, served as an obstacle to progressive change, by preventing the federal government from challenging the separate states in their enforcement of reactionary practices. In particular, it served first (until 1865) as the legal pretext under which slavery was preserved, and later, as a protective shield for other measures whereby civil rights (including voting rights) were infringed upon, if not denied outright, to certain sectors of the population. (The latter practice was outlawed by the federal Voting Rights Act of 1965, but this Act was overturned by the Supreme Court in 2013.)

The biggest institutional rupture in US history was the one brought by the Civil War of 1861-65 – often referred to as the "Second American Revolution." The issue of slavery was of course at the core of this struggle.

---

7 See Greg Palast, *The Best Democracy Money Can Buy* (New York: Seven Stories Press, 2016) and his DVD by the same title (www.gregpalast.com).

But the forces arrayed against the Southern slave-owners were disparate, consisting not only of the enslaved population and its abolitionist allies, but also of capitalist interests seeking to block the extension of slavery into the Western territories (where it was seen as potentially impeding projects for railroad construction). While principled opposition to slavery inspired much of the fighting, capitalist interests remained in command at the national level, and steps toward liberation in the South, after some impressive gains in the immediate postwar years, would be rudely reversed when the federal government, in a pact with the old slave-owning class, withdrew its support for the proclaimed agenda of granting equal rights to the formerly enslaved population.

We shall have more to say later about how the **13th amendment** to the Constitution, which purported to abolish slavery, did not outlaw it completely. The **14th amendment**, which purported to establish equality of all persons before the law, was similarly twisted, as the legal concept of personhood was extended by an 1886 Supreme Court ruling to include *corporations* as "persons." This meant that any right guaranteed to individuals could also be exercised by these much bigger and more powerful entities – a ruling that was applied in the Supreme Court's 2010 decision allowing corporate contributions to candidates for elective office. Similarly, the **15th amendment**, which supposedly guaranteed the right to vote irrespective of "race," nonetheless left the way open to other pretexts for voter-suppression which could be artfully designed with racial parameters in mind – a practice that continues to this day.

Apart from the constitutional obstacles to accountability, there has always been the exceptionally heavy impact of *big money*, in the form of financial contributions to candidates for elective office. Although this is a feature common to all capitalist "democracies," it has taken on extreme proportions in the US for a number of reasons. **First**, the two dominant parties – Republican and Democrat – are alike in being controlled by corporate capitalist interests. The reasons for the failure of a working-class party to become a major player will occupy us in lecture 4, but the effect has been to create a system in which politicians typically compete on the basis of funding from a narrow and relatively privileged sector of the population (some of whose bigger actors – individuals or corporations – contribute to both parties). A **second** factor is the inordinate duration of electoral campaigns. Because of the absolute predictability of the electoral calendar (especially the 4-year presidential term), preparations and fundraising for a given election begin almost as soon as the previous election has been completed. A **third** factor is the purely commercial nature of the mass media, which profit hugely from campaign advertising and would oppose any measures to restrict such advertising for the sake of creating a "level playing field" among candidates. A **fourth** factor is the legal tradition – grounded in corporate "personhood" – that extends free-speech protections to commercial speech (in the form of often huge campaign donations). **Finally**, there is the general culture of acquisitiveness that accords a mix of prestige and vicarious identification to the most extravagant expressions of self-aggrandizement, seeing in them the markers of success.

"Exceptionalism"

This brief survey of governmental structures and their class basis has already highlighted a number of distinctive traits of US society and politics, and it helps explain others. All are more or less directly linked. Among these additional traits are:[8] 1) the pervasive culture of celebrity, glamor, and violence; 2) the exceptionally high proportion of the population that is imprisoned; 3) the vast proliferation of privately owned firearms; 4) the extraordinary incidence of mass shootings by individuals; 5) the astronomical incomes of top corporate management; 6) the highest poverty rate – and the highest obesity rate – among "advanced" countries;[9] 7)

---

8   For details and discussion, see Andrew L. Shapiro, *We're Number One* (New York: Vintage Books, 1992), and Swanson, *Curing Exceptionalism*.

9   As of 2016, the only countries with higher obesity rates than the US were small Pacific island countries and Kuwait. https://obesity.procon.org/view.resource.php?resourceID=00 6032 See Raj Patel, *Stuffed and Starved: The Hidden Battle for the World Food System* (Brooklyn, NY: Melville House, 2007).

tens of millions of people lacking adequate access to healthcare; 8) the highest number of lawyers per capita; 9) the extraordinarily high proportion (over 95%) of criminal charges that are settled without a trial, on the basis of negotiations under duress; and 10) the highest proportion of the population that believes in God.

These traits, especially in combination, indeed make the US "exceptional," although hardly in the way that its official apologists like to pretend. There is much to be said about how the traits mutually reinforce one another. All relate, either directly or indirectly, to the lack of restraint on capitalist power. Capitalist interests, operating either on their own or through the dominant political parties, reward greed, promote individualistic values, skew public discussion, block environmental protections as well as public health and welfare initiatives, encourage scapegoating, and turn a blind eye to abuses of power over vulnerable populations – all along justifying everything with the political rhetoric of a sacred mission, fittingly symbolized with the mantle of world "leadership."

This constellation of traits and practices is not new, but has taken on extreme proportions in the Trump era,[10] as all economic and social ills are ascribed by top officials

---

10 See John Bellamy Foster, *Trump in the White House: Tragedy or Farce* (New York; Monthly Review Press, 2017), and Carl Boggs, *Fascism Old and New: American Politics at the Crossroads* (New York: Routledge, 2018).

either to public-interest-based regulations (which they are systematically dismantling) or to the influx of refugees and the concomitant specter of a nation that no longer has a "white" majority (a scenario they seek to ward off by means of draconian anti-immigrant practices).

Here, continuing our focus on the impact of slavery, I want to situate historically the sudden post-1970s spike in incarceration, which has turned the self-proclaimed flagship of the "free world" into the country with by far the highest proportion of its population ensnared in jails and prisons. We shall examine the prison regime in greater detail in lecture 3; my present concern is to note why and how it came about, and to suggest how it strengthens and helps perpetuate the dominant culture.

The particular circumstances leading to the sudden extreme growth of the prison population arose after 1971, as the relative prosperity that had existed during the period of US economic supremacy following the end of World War II (when the other industrialized countries were temporarily in ruins) came to an abrupt end. An increasing share of US manufacturing industry moved outside the country, leaving major US cities and many former workers in economically depressed conditions.

At the same time, the US ruling class was trying to overcome a serious challenge to its authority as a result of the popular movements of the 1960s and early 1970s – first, against institutional racism, and subsequently against the US military occupation of Vietnam. We shall examine the associated movements further in lecture 4, but the immediate reaction of the ruling class was to take these developments – decried by the influential Harvard professor Samuel P. Huntington as constituting an "excess of democracy"[11] – as signaling a need to dramatically reverse the progressive policies that had been instituted in the 1930s and partly reinforced by the anti-racist legislation of the 1960s.

It was in this context that the Nixon administration (1969-74) initiated the strategy of criminalizing dissent, and that the Reagan administration (1981-89) implemented what would be a continuing assault on welfare services that could otherwise have provided some relief to the victims of deindustrialization.

A related theme throughout this whole period was the "war on drugs." This was an example of a policy which in part reflected real popular concerns, but responded to them in a way that ultimately hurt the victimized communities without addressing the true causes of the problem. Through a bizarre coalition of individuals upset by drug-related street crime in their communities and ruling-class elements seeking to achieve a higher level of control over potentially rebellious populations, a policy of lengthy *mandatory* prison-sentences for drug offenses was introduced. Pursuit and prosecution related to the drug trade then

---

11 Huntington, "The Democratic Distemper," *Public Interest*, no. 41 (Fall, 1975), 36.

became an all-purpose pretext for aggressive policing. As the outlawed substances themselves were widely available, a great deal of discretion was left to the police in deciding whom to target for drug offenses and whom *not* to target. Such decisions could well be guided in part by political and/or race-based criteria.

The mass incarceration that emerged through the convergence of all these factors would have far-reaching effects on US society.[12] At any given moment, approximately 7 million people in the US are under some form of penal supervision (with additional millions of family-members directly affected); among ex-prisoners, an estimated 6 million are permanently disenfranchised under the laws of many of the US states. Moreover, large prison-populations are included in the census-count in rural areas where they are typically held, but are not counted in the urban communities from which they typically come. All this amplifies even further the structural distortions of the electoral process.

The impact goes even further than this, however, and here is where we return to the topic of the dominant culture. One of the deepest effects of mass incarceration is that it perpetuates, reinforces, and legitimizes what Henry A. Giroux has called a "culture of cruelty."[13] I'll

---

12 See Michelle Alexander, *The New Jim Crow: Mass Incarceration in the Age of Colorblindness* (New York: New Press, 2010).
13 Giroux, *America's Addiction to Terrorism* (New York: Monthly Review Press, 2016).

be reminding you of many instances of this culture in the next two lectures, but its most immediately striking manifestation is precisely the phenomenon of the current US president, a quintessential personification of unabashed capitalist greed, who, both despite and because of this, was glamorized by the corporate media long before he became a political candidate; who ran a campaign full of incitement to racist violence; and who is able, despite his contempt for the actual interests of the population, to retain a substantial level of popular support – not a majority, but a large minority, inflated in its impact by the institutional mechanisms we have been looking at.

The media culture that enables this phenomenon is one of unrestrained commercialism. The media are often spoken of, in the US, as the "fourth branch of government" (in addition to the legislature, the executive, and the judiciary). This is no exaggeration. Even though the US media are mostly in private corporate hands, they are indeed the vehicle on which the citizenry primarily depends for its knowledge of what the government is actually doing. According to prevailing ideology, the fact that the media are not owned by the government means that they are independent, and even, in relation to government officials, adversarial – i.e., skeptical and challenging. This is not the way things work, however. There is great conformity and also a strong tendency to quote only official sources on any question on which there's consensus within the ruling class. This applies generally to questions of foreign policy, where a notable example was the way the *New York Times* (the leading national newspaper) cooperated in the government's public campaign to justify in advance the 2003 US invasion of Iraq.

Beyond ideological conformity, the main attributes of the corporate media are their vast dependence on advertising and their devotion to forms of entertainment that make few demands on their audiences. These range from violent to salacious to innocuous, but have in common – whether packaged as news, as talk show, as weather forecast, as sportscast, or as soap opera – the function of serving at once to distract viewers and to reconcile them to the status quo. As part of this process, the media also, despite token concessions to "diversity," continue to foster longstanding racist stereotypes, especially in their crime coverage.[14]

Given that the media indeed operate as a branch of government, one might hope that they could be conceived of in terms of a democratic model – uncovering necessary information, offering well-informed analysis unrestrained by corporate loyalties, and providing wide opportunities for popular

---

14 See Michael Parenti, *Inventing Reality: The Politics of News Media*, 2nd ed. (New York: St. Martin's Press, 1993), and *Make-Believe Media: The Politics of Entertainment* (New York: St. Martin's Press, 1992). For current examples, see http://fair.org/ and its printed newsletter, *Extra!*

participation. There have long been small-scale examples of such a media,[15] but they need to have a much greater presence. What's needed is a participant audience that spans the entire population.

---

15 These range from the "underground" newspapers of the 1960s to such current websites as counterpunch.org, popularresistance.org, therealnews.com, blackagendareport.com, theintercept.com, consortiumnews.com, whowhatwhy.org, truthout.org, truthdig.com, climateandcapitalism.com, mronline.org, democracynow.org, and buildingbridgesradio.org

Lecture 2

US IMPERIALISM: FROM CONTINENTAL EXPANSION TO GLOBAL INTERVENTION

Nation and Empire

Capitalism is inherently an expansionist system. The expansionist thrust was clearly noted by Marx and Engels in the Communist Manifesto, where it was described as a response on the part of capital to the saturation of local markets. Of course, Marx also took into account other dimensions of capitalist expansion, such as perpetual technological innovation. But the competition among the various powers – not only for markets, but for raw materials, for cheap labor-power, for "friendly" foreign regimes, and for lax regulation of such matters as working conditions and environmental discharges – assures that the drive of each capitalist unit to extend the territorial scope of its operations will continue.

My purpose here, though, is to talk not about imperialism in general, but about the particular form it has taken in the US case, leading up to the role that the

US now plays on the global stage, as the country with by far the biggest military arsenal, uniquely spread out over a worldwide network of bases, and with its self-proclaimed entitlement to judge the acceptability of other countries' regimes and, in the case of weaker countries, to intervene unilaterally, whether by CIA "covert operations" or by military force, in an effort to impose – with unpredictable consequences – regimes of its choice.

Imperialism has always entailed military or political domination by great powers over less mighty but more popular forces. First came the conquest of colonies; later came the multilateral military intervention in 1918 against the Russian Revolution. For a number of decades, ending in 1945, imperialism also meant war between rival great powers. After 1945, with the rise of national liberation movements throughout the Third World, the specifically counterrevolutionary thrust of imperialism once again became predominant, especially in Korea and Vietnam but also in Latin America and Southern Africa. In the years since 1989, with the enlarged terrain for capitalist investment created by the collapse of the Soviet Bloc, the counterrevolutionary thrust has become overlaid with a predominant focus on gaining control over regions valued for their natural resources.[1] Because many of these are located in Islamic

---

1 Michael T. Klare, *The Race for What's Left: The Global Scramble for the World's Last Resources* (New York: Metropolitan Books, 2012).

countries (notably, Afghanistan and the Persian Gulf states), the conflict over US control has taken on, in part, the aspect of a struggle over religious identity, as forces throughout the Islamic world have reacted angrily to US military occupation of holy sites and attacks on Muslim populations.

War is currently taking place in many countries occupied by US forces or attacked from the air by US drones or by the bombs of US allies (notably, Israel and Saudi Arabia). What changes will be needed in order for such practice, with its devastating consequences, to be no longer viewed as a routine policy option? While this has always been an important question, it takes on added dimensions at the present time as the Earth's ecological infrastructure collapses into fire and flood, and as 65 million refugees – an unprecedented number – are shunted from one place to another as they search for a home.[2]

To question the political support for a war-oriented agenda is to inquire into the cycle whereby, despite the high costs of war even within the US, there nonetheless remains a critical mass of the domestic population that embodies and perpetuates the culture of militarism – not only in its opinions and its voting behavior, but also in its actual conduct (for example, assaults on members of ethnic, cultural, religious or sexual minorities; mass

---

2 On the refugee crisis, see Ai Weiwei's documentary film *Human Flow* (2017).

shootings). What alternative model can be put forward for the way the government of a major power can conduct itself on the world stage? And what dialectic can we identify between the practice of a major-power government and matching or complementary behaviors on the part of its individual citizens?

Particularities of the US Case

The distinctive features of US imperialism are: 1) its integral relationship to the formation of the nation-state itself; 2) how it was marked from the outset by extreme doctrines of racial supremacy; 3) the circumstance of its emergence as a late challenger to European empires, moving territorially only against the decaying Spanish Empire and otherwise preferring to issue proclamations rather than establish its own colonial administrations; 4) the way it sought to cloak itself with an ideological claim comparing the American colonies' 18th-century war of independence to modern anti-colonial struggles, while asserting that the US itself is not a colonizing power; 5) how it eventually took on an unprecedented role as worldwide enforcer of imperial/capitalist interests.

(1) The US national territory was formed by waging wars of conquest against indigenous nations and against Mexico. The original US flag was designed with one star and one stripe for each of the original 13 colonies, but by an 1818 Act of Congress, it became the regular

practice – globally unprecedented – to add a new star with the incorporation of each new state, thereby making the flag a visual tally of the nation's territorial expansion.

Especially for the conquest of indigenous lands, but also for controlling the enslaved population within already-established states, heavy reliance was placed on private armed operatives or *vigilantes*. The federal government paid rewards ("bounties") to individuals who killed Indians, based on physical evidence of the numbers of their victims. The tradition of an armed (male) citizenry gained general acceptance and was enshrined in the 2nd amendment to the US Constitution. This became particularly important on the so-called "frontier," where the armed citizens constituted an advance guard for the subjugation of Indian peoples.

It was understood that the status of citizen applied only to those of European descent. Arms were routinely used by them not only for conquest but also to settle disputes within their own community. This practice, together with the activities of the Ku Klux Klan (founded in the Southern states after the Civil War to terrorize the formerly enslaved black population and keep it in a state of submission), formed the basis for the notorious national "gun culture" which now is much bewailed but little restrained, as the psychology it promotes – "Shoot first; ask questions later!" – is consistent with that required for officially promoted military interventions around the world.[3]

(2) Policies of annihilation applied against indigenous peoples in North America were re-applied, with similar (explicitly racist) rationales, in the US conquest of the Philippines (1898-1902). They would later again be applied on a massive scale, notably in the use of atomic bombs against Japan in 1945 and in the massacres committed by US aerial and occupation forces – totaling in the millions – in both Korea and Vietnam.

In reflecting on this awful history, one has to recognize that the US is not the only imperial power that has carried out such atrocities. Massacres committed over the years by European forces in Africa and South Asia, by Japanese forces in China (especially in 1937), and by Germany's Nazi regime against Jews and other targeted populations in Europe (1941-45) must not be forgotten. What has evolved, however, is a situation in which the US, as further discussed below, has now become the de facto command-center of global imperialism, continuing under its own initiative – though supported especially by Israel and Saudi Arabia – practices which in other advanced capitalist regimes have come under more criticism.

---

[3] See Roxanne Dunbar-Ortiz, *Loaded: A Disarming History of the Second Amendment* (San Francisco: City Lights Books, 2018).

The distinctive US role in this respect finds its domestic counterpart in the practice of capital punishment, which has been abolished in other advanced capitalist countries (where the culture of working-class parties has had a stronger influence than in the US). The death penalty preserves symbolically the culture of conquest, which in turn ideologically fuels the global military agenda. In its application, which disproportionately targets people of color, the death penalty reinforces, consistently with US military training, the racist impulse to treat the enemy or the social outcast as less than human. The culminating expression of this urge to obliterate the "other" is the readiness of US leaders to brandish the "ultimate weapon." Although there are several national governments that possess nuclear bombs, the US is the only one that not only has dropped them on people, but has frequently and now increasingly used them to issue threats, and has also insistently claimed the prerogative to launch a "first strike" (i.e., to use its nuclear arsenal not as a deterrent but as offensive weapons). US officials who recently withdrew from the international treaty on Iran indicated clearly, in so doing, their readiness to carry out a potentially nuclear attack on that country. The ease with which they can contemplate such an extreme step is in tune with a long and constantly reinforced tradition of denying the full humanity of those whom they view as obstacles to their imperial designs and whom they then typically categorize – whether by physical or by cultural traits – as "other," whose lives they consequently treat as worthless.[4]

(3) The US claimed Latin America as its sphere of interest, to the exclusion of other great powers (Monroe Doctrine, 1823), without seeking formal colonial rule. The only acknowledged US colonization was that of the Philippines, whose conquest included massacres on a par with those committed against the Indians in the course of continental expansion. Other conquered territories were officially incorporated into the US (as "territories" and not, except for Hawaii, as states), with their residents being accorded US citizenship.

The US early took on the self-assigned role of spokesperson for other imperial powers when it put forward in 1899 its Open Door policy toward China, in which it laid down the principle of equal access of all foreign powers to the Chinese market. The US also claimed the prerogative to occupy countries militarily, sometimes for years (e.g., in the Caribbean), in pursuit of particular objectives ("protecting US interests").

(4) Although the American colonies' war of independence was in the nature of a separatist secession rather than a revolt by a conquered population, the

---

4 See Frantz Fanon, *The Wretched of the Earth* (New York: Grove Press, 1963) and Edward Said, *Orientalism* (New York: Vintage Books, 1978, 2003).

rhetoric of the precipitating grievances (such as protests against British taxes) would later be cited by the US as a basis for claiming legitimacy as an anti-colonial power. This tradition would inform official rationales given for US intervention in 1898 in the Cuban war for independence from Spain – even though the US goal was to replace Spain as the dominant power rather than to support the Cuban insurgents. Nonetheless, the Vietnamese national liberation movement in 1945 invoked the American Declaration of Independence as an inspiration for their own struggle against French rule, hoping to gain US support. But the US government was unmoved.

The most conspicuous example of the US's pretense at disavowing imperialism has been its denial that Puerto Rico is a US colony. This claim is based on the fact that Puerto Ricans are US citizens (a status granted in 1917 to justify drafting them into the US armed forces); however, in order to be allowed to vote in US elections, they must establish residence in one of the 50 US States. Moreover, although Puerto Rico has a local governing apparatus, its finances are entirely controlled by the US Congress.[5]

(5) The US claims the prerogative to intervene militarily in other countries not on the basis of any

---

5 See Nelson A. Denis, *War Against All Puerto Ricans: Revolution and Terror in America's Colony* (New York: Nation Books, 2015).

formal authority to rule a given territory, but rather on the basis of more general "security" criteria (often articulated in the language of human rights concerns), which it invokes wherever and whenever it chooses. The doctrine under which it does so was formally proclaimed in 1947 and was re-invoked in 2002. In support of this doctrine, "the United States has approximately 800 formal military bases in 80 countries, a number that could exceed 1,000 if you count troops stationed at embassies and missions,… with some 138,000 soldiers stationed around the globe."[6]

The 1947 declaration, known as the Truman Doctrine, was in response to the political threat posed by world socialist revolution. It asserted a US commitment to defend "free peoples everywhere" against what it described as a form of aggression threatening them from without. The rationale for US imperial policies was thus formulated explicitly in global terms, abjuring any claim to establish a specifically US sphere of interest but yet nonetheless putting forward a notion of "freedom" that corresponded exactly to the hegemonic US understanding of this concept, which insisted above all on the free operations of capital.[7] By 2002, with the

---

[6] Alice Slater, "The US Has Military Bases in 80 Countries," *The Nation*, January 24, 2018.

[7] See Thomas McCormick, *America's Half-Century: United States Foreign Policy in the Cold War and After*, 2nd ed. (Baltimore: Johns Hopkins University Press, 1995).

threat of revolution seeming less immediate, the new rationale for imperial intervention, put forward by President Bush Jr., became the threat of "terrorism" – which he viewed as an unprovoked assault on "Western values" and not as what it was, namely, a reaction to hostile economic and military impositions.

How US imperialism justifies itself

The US ruling class claims an entitlement to world leadership. This leadership is tightly linked to the interests of capital. And yet the rulers cast their claim to leadership in moralistic terms, the broadest of which is the assertion that its purpose is to uphold freedom and democracy.[8] One has to wonder how anyone can take such a claim seriously in view of the actual practice of such close US allies as Saudi Arabia – surely one of the most despotic regimes on the planet.[9] But the dominant political/media complex of the US creates its own reality, whereby democratic credentials are seen to depend not on a regime's accountability and service to its own people, but rather on the degree to which it accepts

---

8   See Eric Foner, *Who Owns History? Rethinking the Past in a Changing World* (New York: Hill & Wang, 2002), 58-74; also Noam Chomsky and C.J. Polychroniou, *Optimism over Despair: On Capitalism, Empire, and Social Change* (Chicago: Haymarket, 2017).

9   See Medea Benjamin, *Kingdom of the Unjust: Behind the U.S.-Saudi Connection* (New York: OR Books, 2016).

capitalist priorities and allies itself with the US in the international arena.

The obfuscation of reality by US opinion-makers sometimes attains comical proportions. They denounce governments for interfering in the affairs of other countries when this is precisely what the US government itself does – on a far larger scale, and increasingly unapologetically – all the time. The US media have for many months now been embroiled in speculation based on unsupported assertions by Intelligence officials to the effect that Russian advertising on Facebook played a decisive role in determining the outcome of the 2016 US presidential election. Any possible impact of such alleged targeting is dwarfed, however, by the undisputed and overwhelming role that the US played in the 1996 Russian election, when it deployed vast resources to assure the re-election of the highly unpopular incumbent president, Boris Yeltsin.[10]

Corresponding to the double standard in official propaganda – its practice of exaggerating the international role of US adversaries (like Russia or Iran) while not mentioning, in the same context, the

---

10 *Time*, cover story, July 15, 1996, http://content.time.com/time/covers/0,16641,19960715,00.html. See, more generally, works by William Blum, including his online *Anti-Empire Report*. For critique of the "intelligence" assertions, see the article by former US Ambassador to Russia, Jack F. Matlock, Jr., "Amid 'Russiagate' Hysteria, What Are the Facts?" *The Nation*, June 1, 2018.

overwhelming global interventionist presence of the US – is a real blindness to reality on the part of significant sectors of public opinion. Not only are people in these sectors uninformed; they have no wish to be informed. It does not even occur to them – except sometimes momentarily, on the basis of quickly buried news reports – that the US could itself be viewed as a threat to peace, or (in language often used by US officials) as a "rogue state."[11]

The view of the US as the principal threat to peace is indeed widely held in other parts of the world, but significant numbers of Americans, beyond not being aware of this, tend not to care what the rest of the world thinks.[12] Believing official rhetoric, they presume that US armed forces are in other countries on some kind of benevolent mission. Such credulity often depends on having short historical memories. For example, in the case of Afghanistan, the US, beginning in 1978, mobilized Islamic fundamentalists to overthrow a (Soviet-supported) regime which had provided for the education of women and girls. Later, after the successor regime of Islamists had turned against the US (following the US's 1990 troop deployment to Saudi Arabia), the US

---

11 See William Blum, *Rogue State: A Guide to the World's Only Superpower* (Monroe, ME: Common Courage Press, 2000).

12 In a recent public opinion survey, 39% preferred that the US be respected for its military might, rather than being liked for its policies. Swanson, *Curing Exceptionalism*, 149.

switched to defining *them* as the enemy. The US then began claiming that an important goal of its occupying forces was to liberate women[13] -- which did not stop it from supporting local warlords like Gulbuddin Hikmatyar, who was known to have ordered the disfiguring of unveiled women by having acid thrown in their faces.[14]

The mindset of the constituency that accepts US imperialism encompasses a mixture of partly clashing principles and observations. On the one hand, the government has to maintain the pretense that US military missions are directed at helping the local populations. On the other hand, the idea that local populations might have something to say about the kind of help that would be useful to them is never considered. Least of all does it occur to this constituency that the best way the US could help local populations would be to give up the extraordinarily presumptuous and violent project of suppressing their insurgencies and shaping their governments.

The absurdities that issue from the assumptions of this constituency can be quite striking. The assumption of US "good intentions" runs deep, extending even to

---

13 See Hester Eisenstein, *Feminism Seduced: How Global Elites Use Women's Labor and Ideas to Exploit the World* (Boulder, CO: Paradigm Publishers, 2009).

14 Mahmood Mamdani, *Good Muslim, Bad Muslim: America, the Cold War, and the Roots of Terror* (New York: Pantheon Books, 2004), 144.

many who might otherwise be open to criticizing US practices; it is the fallback claim that is made in retrospect about policies whose outcomes have clearly been disastrous. Many who lament the outcome of the US invasion of Vietnam – although in some cases only because of its military failures – nonetheless say that the war was undertaken for a "noble purpose" – which in effect signifies ratifying in retrospect the false justifications that were given for entering it.

The US government justified the invasion at the time – in the early 1960s – by making the false claim that the Southern half of that country had been "invaded" by outside forces from the North, when in fact there was a broadly supported liberation movement within the South against the unpopular US-installed regime. This information at first became known to the US public only through the reporting of dissident journalists like Wilfred Burchett and I.F. Stone, and via radical publications like the *National Guardian*. It would later be massively confirmed, however, by the direct experience of US troops who learned for themselves, in some cases at a high personal cost, how popular were the forces that they had been sent to fight against.[15]

---

15 On the revolt of US troops in Vietnam, see David Zeiger's documentary film, *Sir, No Sir!* (2005). The *National Guardian* (in its later years, *Guardian*) was a weekly newspaper published from 1948 to 1992. I.F. Stone produced his own weekly (later bi-weekly) newsletter from 1953 to 1971.

No less disastrous in its outcome has been the US-initiated war in Iraq, from the continuous bombings begun in 1991 to the invasion of 2003 and beyond. The official lies that led up to the 2003 invasion have long since been admitted by those who told them, but even as the after-shocks of the US occupation continue (notably, in the formation and international operations of the terrorist group ISIS), there has been shockingly little public discussion of US responsibility for triggering those effects.

There is a common perception that, given an intractable situation of conflict in some country (not to mention cases where a regime openly defies capitalist priorities), it is incumbent upon the US to "do something" about it, and the only readily available guise of that "something" is a military action, which has the threefold advantage, from the standpoint of the US political leadership, of (a) being highly visible, (b) showing US power and effectiveness (at least in the short run), and (c) providing an opportunity to "justify" the enormous US military budget.

As disturbing as the failure to recognize US responsibility for the disastrous condition in which Iraq and its neighbors now find themselves is the more general attitude of political impunity, manifested most remarkably in the refusal of President Obama to prosecute officials of the preceding Bush Jr. administration for their violations of US and international law regarding torture.

Just as there is a double standard regarding foreign intervention – seen as good (or else not even noticed) when the US does it to others, yet condemned in the most self-righteous tones in the event that others would do it to "us" – so also there is a double standard regarding the response to torture: For those who order and carry out a program of torture, all possible leniency is applied, and they may even qualify for promotion; on the other hand, those who reveal or confirm the practice of torture – such as Chelsea Manning and John Kiriakou – must be severely punished.

The problem is thus defined not as one of the actual *deeds* of the government, but rather as one of *image*: it is assumed that "we" are "good," and it is acknowledged that torture is "bad." But what if "we" commit torture? Since "we" are "good," that is not admissible; consequently, those who make it known are disclosing forbidden information, and must therefore suffer exemplary reprisals.

A note on recent history

Countless instances of imperialist intervention could be presented. There is no better survey, for the 1945-2003 period, than the 55 tightly written and fully documented chapters of William Blum's book, *Killing Hope: US Military and CIA Interventions since World War II.*[16]

---

16 (Monroe, ME: Common Courage Press, 2003).

I have strong personal memories of some of these episodes, having been early involved in protests against US attempts to destroy the Cuban Revolution, and having later lived for more than a year in Chile, which between 1970 and 1973 underwent the noteworthy experience of having the first government with a serious project of socialist transformation elected to office within a bourgeois constitutional framework, only to be overthrown by a military coup – predictably, and with US complicity despite the latter's pretense to democratic values – before the process could be carried to completion. It was in relation to the Chilean socialist project that President Nixon's National Security adviser Henry Kissinger gave his unforgettable advice on sabotaging the process, which so many local activists had worked for years to put in place. Contending that Chile should "not be allowed to go communist through the irresponsibility of its people," Kissinger told Nixon that the US, by cutting off all credit lines to Chile, should "make the economy scream."

I also had first-hand experience of the Sandinista Revolution in Nicaragua, where I spent time during the election of 1984. This was another case where a process launched with great popular support – and with much initial success in bringing basic services to the people – was subjected to unrelenting assaults by US-organized exile forces, which eventually wore down the project to the point where most of the popular initiatives were destroyed and the old financial elites recovered most of their power.

The current crisis in Venezuela shows traces of both the Chilean and the Nicaraguan precedents. Certainly the lies told about it by the US leadership are in the same tradition – of denying that a process is democratic when the results to which it leads challenge the power of the local ruling class and foreign economic interests.[17] These and many other cases offer ample material for reflection.

What I would come back to reflect on at this point, however, is the whole idea of a "war on terror," which has been the 21st-century continuation of the earlier crusade against communism. The turning point of the 1990s needs to be revisited. Before the collapse of the Soviet Bloc, the whole justification given by the US government for its huge military budget and its many foreign interventions was that everything was directed against the "Soviet threat." When this "threat" – which US experts knew to be political rather than military,[18]

---

17 US sanctions on Venezuela have effectively made "the economy scream"--https://popularresistance.org/blockading-venezuela-the-linchpin-of-the-us-strategy-of-aggression/ For sustained coverage of the Venezuelan process, see https://venezuelanalysis.com/

18 This awareness is documented in the foundational statement of US Cold War policy, George F. Kennan's anonymously published 1947 article, "The Sources of Soviet Conduct" (http://www.historyguide.org/Europe/Kennan.html), which

although they did not say this publicly – suddenly dissolved, people could be forgiven for imagining that a new era of peace might open up.

On the contrary, the disappearance of the militarily strongest adversary to the US meant that the US government could now impose its interventionist agenda with much less concern about possible adverse consequences. The first major action undertaken by President Bush Sr. after the fall of the Berlin Wall (November 1989) was to invade Panama. In August 1990, he gave a non-negotiable ultimatum to Iraq, leading to decades of bombardment starting in January 1991. The subsequent US invasion of Iraq (2003) followed upon the terrorist attacks of 9/11 (2001) in New York and Washington. Insiders in the administration of President Bush Jr. who, through their organization, the Project for the New American Century, had since at least 1997 been calling for the overthrow of the Iraqi government (which they considered too independent), took those attacks, on the basis of no evidence, as the excuse they needed for invading not only Afghanistan but Iraq as well.[19] The 9/11 attacks gave

---

evokes a systemic challenge and nowhere alludes to military invasion as a component of Soviet strategy.

19 Afghanistan was targeted not because of any logistical evidence of complicity in 9/11 but allegedly because it was the home base of leading Islamist Osama bin Laden; however, US forces continued to occupy Afghanistan for years after their 2011 assassination of bin Laden (by which time he was in Pakistan).

them a pretext for calling the entire US military mission in the Islamic world a "war on terror."

Of course, this phrase is absurd. Insofar as particular acts of terrorism are carried out by non-state operatives, they are a response from among peoples without national armies to attacks carried out on their communities by armies equipped with the most sophisticated weaponry. If the well equipped armies subsequently carry out even more attacks (in their "war on terror"), then even more people in the affected communities will draw the conclusion that their only recourse is to engage in terroristic acts on their own part.

We see here again the extraordinary mix of blindness and double standards in the imperialist ideology. It recognizes the phenomenon of terror – attacks on civilians – only when these are carried out against its own people, and not when the imperialist power (or its surrogates) rains down a similar terror on people in the targeted countries.[20]

The underlying interests served by imperialism are of course economic. But the devaluation of persons is part

---

Iraq was never linked in any way with the 9/11 attacks. The principal external actor in the attacks was Saudi Arabia, which had conspicuous ties to the Bush Jr. administration. The official US inquiry into the attacks was tightly circumscribed. See David Ray Griffin and Elizabeth Woodworth, *9/11 Unmasked: An International Review Panel Investigation* (Interlink Books, 2018).

20 See Ellen Ray and William H. Schaap, eds., *Covert Action: The Roots of Terrorism* (Melbourne and New York: Ocean Press, 2003).

of the means by which the economic goals are pursued. What the dynamic unleashed by the "war on terror" demonstrates is that imperialism tends toward a perpetual escalation in levels of violence. The only alternative is to reject the acquisitive impulse that drives the process from the outset. This is where the critique of capitalism comes into play, now given even greater urgency by the environmental crisis.

Lecture 3

FROM SLAVERY TO MASS INCARCERATION: THE SAGA OF AFRICAN-DESCENDED PEOPLE IN THE UNITED STATES

Racism and imperialism

We need to explore in greater depth the factors that have given the US global role its distinctive character in comparison with previous empires.

We have already noted the link between forms of domination inside and outside the national territory. Racism and imperialism are of a piece. Both are grounded in material interest but at the same time have a psychological dimension. While the psychological dimension – the subjective affirmation of superiority – does not "explain" either phenomenon, it plays a vital role in giving both of them (racism and imperialism), within the majority populations of the countries in which they originate, an appearance of democratic legitimacy.

It also has the effect of producing a feeling of entitlement on the part of the perpetrators, who then presume that they have a moral justification, echoing the crusading rhetoric of opinion-leaders, for the ravages they commit – from brutalizing and enslaving people (or denying them equal rights) to imposing "regime change" on countries whose governments they disapprove of.

The material interest underlying both racism and imperialism is that of the capitalist ruling class. Both racism and imperialism entail super-exploitation of a particular, "racially" defined sector of the working class, and both create divisions among workers who, were it not for the arbitrary intrusion of racial ideology, would be able to see that they share a common class interest. To the extent that this ideology prevails, however, workers outside the super-exploited sector are pressured at every moment to assume that their interests lie in accepting a social agenda defined by the ruling class.

Imperialistic super-patriotism and the doctrine of white supremacy blind their working-class adherents to the sacrifices that are being imposed on them – which range from cutbacks of social services to the more direct consequences of imperialist war. These include not only the risk of life and limb to those mobilized for military service, but also widespread mental disorder, social breakdown, and a politics of fear, rationalized by constant talk of the possibility – real or imagined – of armed reprisals (terrorist attacks) from imperialism's victims. This fear then in turn becomes a pretext for repressive policies directed especially at those victims, at home as well as abroad. We see the same dynamic that I noted earlier regarding the "war on terror": In both cases, there is a self-fulfilling prophecy entailing a permanent cycle of suspicion and violence.

Slavery and its legacy

Slavery took on a particularly virulent form in the US. To a greater extent than in earlier slave societies, US practice, from its origins in the cramped dungeons of slave-ships, entailed an agenda of total suppression of human faculties, as illustrated by the criminalization of literacy – making it a felony to teach an enslaved person how to read and write. The slave-masters posited an inherent or "racial" difference between Africans and Europeans. This did not stop them from impregnating their African female slaves. The offspring of such coercive unions were in turn kept as slaves, thereby enlarging the slave-master's patrimony. In order to maintain, despite such practice, the legal and cultural fiction of fundamentally distinct "races," they had to adopt a definition of blackness whereby it was not a function of actual skin color (or other genetic traits), but was rather, for any given individual, the outcome of having just a single ancestor – in some cases, a rather remote one – who was African.

This definition carried over into the period after slavery was formally abolished (by the 13th amendment to the US Constitution) in 1865. On the one hand, that amendment contained an "exception clause," whereby the legal termination of slavery would not apply to persons convicted of crimes. On the other hand, a whole battery of petty offenses was legislated into existence in the Southern states, with the intention that they would be enforced only against blacks, who would then be compelled to submit to forced labor (typically, agricultural labor or roadwork performed by chain-gangs – groups of prisoners chained together by their ankles).[1] And in case there would be any possible defiance of this updated labor regime, a reign of terror was instituted, spearheaded by the Ku Klux Klan, which included frequent lynchings – both spontaneous and pre-arranged (the latter publicly announced in the form of news-stories in local papers) – as punishment for even the most minimal expression – or even appearance – of insubordination (e.g., failure of a black person to use

---

[1] These sets of laws were known as the Black Codes. The underlying idea of deliberately creating a captive labor force is perpetuated in the 21st-century California practice of blocking decarceration in order maintain a reserve pool of prisoners to fight forest fires at slave wages, thereby saving the state up to $100 million per year. https://www.democracynow.org/2018/9/12/

terms of respect – "sir" or "ma'am" – in addressing a white person).[2]

What changes, what stays the same?-1

The essential social relationship of slavery was thus preserved even though its legal regime was supposedly ended. This pattern of giving lip-service to a change while at the same time undermining it in practice would be replicated in many areas of policy and would clearly be perpetuated in the context of race relations.

The most general level at which one can see this dynamic is in relation to the preservation of class rule across periods of history. Given an appropriate institutional framework, a dominant class can relinquish certain expressions of its power while at the same time finding new ways to assure that its compromises do not reduce the core of its strength. At one time, for example, it was feared that universal suffrage would bring an end to the power of the privileged class. But through a combination of financial, cultural, and ideological practices, as well as concessions on secondary matters (for example, acceptance of labor unions and of unemployment insurance), the concentration of power remained undiminished. Moreover, with this economic and social power remaining intact, the concessions

---

[2] The Legacy Museum: From Slavery to Mass Incarceration, which opened in 2018 in Montgomery, Alabama, provides vivid documentation of these practices.

could, at opportune moments, be weakened and in some cases even rescinded.

The preservation of a racist structure in the US has been closely tied to the preservation of class rule.³ The new reign of terror that arose in the Southern states after the formal ending of slavery was directed above all at controlling black labor and preventing any possible working-class alliance across racial lines (of which there were some indications in the immediate aftermath of the Civil War, during the brief period known as Radical Reconstruction).⁴ But the institution of lynching – which was initially applied to block the extension of voting rights under the 15th amendment – served not only to terrorize black people; by its public and even festive character, it fostered complicity and conformity in the white population. The laws imposing racial segregation were thus reinforced by the dominant culture, and could easily be seen (by people growing up within that culture) as reflecting a "natural" order.

It was not until the 1960s that these state laws were finally overruled by federal legislation. A massive popular movement was required in order to bring about this change. Although small-scale local and individual acts of resistance to segregation took place throughout the

---

3 See Manning Marable, *How Capitalism Underdeveloped Black America* (Chicago: Haymarket, 2015 [1983]).
4 W.E.B. Du Bois, *Black Reconstruction in America* (New York: Harcourt, Brace, 1935).

preceding period,[5] the challenge had to come eventually at a national level. The early steps in this process were the labor organizing efforts mounted in the South, beginning in the 1920s, by the Communist Party, which was the only non-black organization that took a proactive approach to recruiting black people into political work.[6] It was the CP's efforts that laid the groundwork for the later civil rights movement. (Correspondingly, the overtly racist Southern politicians were the most intransigent anticommunists; their defense of segregation included routinely referring to "race-mixing" as a "communist" strategy designed to "weaken America.")

The stability of segregationist structures was severely shaken by US participation in World War II, for which the public rationale was the need to crush regimes founded on doctrines of racial supremacy. The irony of fighting in such a war while being assigned to racially segregated military units was inescapable.[7] This contributed to a heightened level of anti-racist organizing in the postwar period, beginning within black

---

5   Robin D.G. Kelley, *Race Rebels: Culture, Politics, and the Black Working Class* (New York: Free Press, 1994).

6   Robin D.G. Kelley, *Hammer and Hoe: Alabama Communists during the Great Depression* (Chapel Hill: University of North Carolina Press, 1990).

7   See Nelson Peery's autobiographical account in his *Black Fire: The Making of an American Revolutionary* (New York: New Press, 1994).

communities in the South. Given the vulnerability of these communities, it was important to attract into their campaigns white participants, who came mostly from other parts of the country. Two additional conditions further facilitated the federal government's eventual willingness to move against the Southern authorities. One was the international condemnation to which the US was exposed. The other is the fact that in the preceding decades, millions of black people had migrated out of the South, thereby significantly reducing their weight as a potential voting bloc in the Southern states.

The high points of the struggle for civil rights have been widely recounted, beginning with the 1955 Montgomery bus-boycott – against racially segregated seating on public buses – and culminating in the 1965 Selma-to-Montgomery march in support of voting rights. That ten-year period was one of continuous organizing, often including civil disobedience actions, in some cases by racially integrated groups, in defiance of race-based restrictions on public services. It also included a continuous process of political education – both one-on-one and in "freedom schools" – and campaigns of voter-registration.

It is important to emphasize that all these efforts were conducted against a background of physical danger. Civil rights workers were routinely subject to assault (by vigilantes as well as police), and scores of them were killed. Martin Luther King, Jr. was of course a key figure, although the actual work of organizing was done especially by young people belonging to the Student Nonviolent Coordinating Committee (SNCC). King's approach of strategic nonviolence was helpful in gaining official acceptance for the movement's immediate demands, which centered on ending legal segregation. But even while the movement was still growing, many of its local activists prepared discreetly for armed self-defense against vigilante attacks.[8] And King himself, when the major legislative victories had been won, recognized that those victories were insufficient to assure the satisfaction of broader popular needs.

This recognition had been a starting point for Malcolm X, whose base was in the North, where segregation was not enshrined in law but where a vast racial gulf nonetheless existed in terms of social conditions. Malcolm began as a Black Nationalist but evolved in 1963 toward a more internationalist position, with a strong recognition of the economic dimension of racist structures. His strategy and that of King were approaching convergence at the time of their single brief meeting in March 1964. After the assassination of Malcolm (1965), King moved increasingly toward a structural analysis and a comprehensive critique of US society, including a decisive condemnation (in 1967) of the US war in Vietnam. His next major project, to

---

8 See August H. Nimtz, "Violence and/or Nonviolence in the Success of the Civil Rights Movement: The Malcolm X-Martin Luther King, Jr. Nexus," *New Political Science*, 38:1 (March 2016).

organize a national campaign around the labor demands of sanitation workers, was terminated in 1968 by his assassination.

By this time, SNCC and other activists had already begun to move beyond any demand that seemed to entail integration into the US mainstream, and to call instead for Black Power, meaning, above all, self-determination of their own community. A new major force arose in 1966 with the formation, initially in Oakland, California, of the Black Panther Party (BPP).[9] The BPP began, in the tradition of Malcolm X, with a call for armed self-defense in response to police violence. But it also organized community services – including breakfast for school children and free clinics – and popularized a structural (anti-capitalist) understanding of racist oppression. Its call for "power to the people" was non-racial, and its charismatic young Chicago organizer, Fred Hampton, pioneered the idea of a "rainbow coalition" that would include all oppressed groups, of every ethnicity. Hampton too, however, was assassinated (in December 1969).

---

9 See Kathleen Cleaver and George Katsiaficas, eds., *Liberation, Imagination, and the Black Panther Party* (New York: Routledge, 2001).

A note on assassinations

It is important at this point to insert a note about the key role of assassinations in shaping the course of the country during this whole period. We considered in lecture 1 some of the many legal devices – whether in the constitution, in legislative acts, or in judicial rulings – that serve to block or distort the representation of popular demands in the US. We have also noted the role of the corporate media in obstructing access to necessary information and analysis. Assassinations constitute a different and more terrifying obstacle to democracy. Being less predictable at any given moment (compared to the functioning of the various "branches of government"), they are typically viewed not as part of the governing structure at all, but rather as a kind of random external intrusion. They are in most cases attributed to isolated ("lone wolf") individuals, but there is in every such case a great deal of reluctance on the part of officialdom to pursue any serious investigation of the crime (i.e., any investigation that goes beyond seeking confirmation of the quickly announced official story). This very reluctance can itself be seen as constituting a structural pattern.

The case in which the underlying reality has been most irrefutably disclosed (although only after many years) is that of Fred Hampton.[10] It was conclusively

---

[10] Jeffrey Haas, *The Assassination of Fred Hampton* (Chicago: Lawrence Hill, 2010).

shown that the police action against him – firing a fusillade of bullets through the door of his apartment in the middle of the night – was carried out under direct orders from the Federal Bureau of Investigation (FBI). The evidence in the other major cases – not only Martin Luther King and Malcolm X, but also President John F. Kennedy (in 1963) and presidential candidate Robert F. Kennedy (JFK's brother) (in 1968) – could be the subject of lengthy expositions, but enough research has now been done in all these cases to thoroughly discredit the officially promulgated narratives of the killings. In terms of the structures and practices that underlie this pattern, I consider the most valuable exposé to be that of the investigative journalist David Talbot in his magisterial biography of Allen Dulles.[11]

The political importance of each of these assassinations is itself a topic of major interest. Obviously, a certain amount of speculation is involved in such assessments. But in the cases of Malcolm X, Martin Luther King, Jr., and Fred Hampton, it is clear from widely publicized internal documents that the FBI

---

11 David Talbot, *The Devil's Chessboard: Allen Dulles, the CIA, and the Rise of America's Secret Government* (New York: HarperCollins, 2015), 494-586, 610-613, provides enough evidence on the assassinations of both the Kennedy brothers to conclusively discredit the hypothesis of lone killers. On the King assassination, for which key evidence was belatedly aired in court, see William F. Pepper, *The Plot to Kill King* (New York: Skyhorse Publishing, 2016).

viewed all three as capable of galvanizing a major revolutionary movement, and saw this as a danger – a threat to "national security" – to be avoided at all costs.[12] The FBI's assessment reflects the fact that all three leaders, while strongly rooted in the black community, were expressing perspectives that addressed a wider audience as well, in their recognition of class issues and in the extension of their critique to encompass the ruling class's foreign policy agenda as well as its domestic policies.

What changes, what stays the same?–2

The murder of Fred Hampton was only the most spectacular of many measures taken to destroy the Black Panther Party. Given the wide popular support that the BPP had built up through its community programs, the longer-term official response had to include some way of depoliticizing the communities. There could be no more effective way to do this than through creating conditions for internecine conflict and responding with an overwhelming police presence. As we noted in lecture 1, this was made possible by the War on Drugs. The deliberate nature of that war – as well as its wider political significance – was expressed in a comment made by President Nixon to one of his aides, to the effect that (as

---

12 Ward Churchill and Jim Vander Wall, eds., *The COINTELPRO Papers: Documents from the FBI's Secret Wars Against Dissent in the United States* (Cambridge, MA: South End Press, 2002), 123-164.

the aide paraphrased it) "you have to face the fact that the whole problem is the blacks. The key is to devise a system that recognizes this while not appearing to."[13] The development of this "system" would be fostered not only by the criminalization of drug trafficking, but also by direct complicity on the part of the government in flooding the black community with drugs.[14]

With the War on Drugs, and, as its offshoot, the world's highest incarceration rate, we once again encounter a phenomenon peculiar to the US, unlike anything in other advanced capitalist countries. The drug-war complex thus takes its place, in its "exceptional" character, alongside the gun culture, the Southern lynch mobs, and the pro-capitalist leadership of the major labor organizations. In all these domains, we find the ironic scenario of a sector of the working-class or oppressed populations endorsing or even promoting, sometimes with great eagerness, the agenda of the capitalist ruling class. In the case of the War on Drugs, the historic timing of its initiation was decisive. The mid-1970s was a period in which, as a result of the civil rights laws, including the Voting Rights Act of 1965, new opportunities were opening up for black politicians, especially at the local level. Along with this came

---

13 H.R. Haldeman, *Diaries*, quoted in Alexander, *The New Jim Crow*, 44.

14 Gary Webb, *Dark Alliance: The CIA, the Contras, and the Crack Cocaine Explosion* (New York: Seven Stories Press, 1999).

demands for the entry of black officers into the police force and even – especially in black-majority cities like Washington, D.C. – into the position of police chief. At the same time, economic conditions in the black neighborhoods were abysmal, leading many of their more desperate residents, young men especially, into drug dealing, turf warfare, and what was widely labeled "black on black" crime. The ironic result is that pressure to have a greater police presence – and to establish draconian prison sentences for drug-related offenses – came from voices (especially those of mothers and older people) from within the very constituencies that would later be drastically disempowered by those steps.[15]

The net effect of all this can be seen as a partial reenactment of what happened in the late 19th century, after the end of the Civil War. At that time the measures taken to establish equal rights were nullified in the Southern states through the institution of the legal regime of segregation, backed by the terror of lynch mobs. Now, in the late 20th century, the gains brought by the civil rights movement came under a somewhat different type of assault, but with no less of an impact on the majority of the black population.[16] The big difference

---

15 James Forman, Jr., *Locking Up Our Own: Crime and Punishment in Black America* (New York: Farrar, Straus & Giroux, 2017).

16 This historical parallel is brought out in Steve Martinot, "Probing the Epidemic of Police Murders," *Socialism and Democracy*, 27:1 (March 2013).

in more recent years lies in the entry of a significant number of African American individuals into the higher reaches of government. But, as the role of such persons in relation to the drug war suggests, this does not necessarily signify an improvement for the black population as a whole. Moreover, the conspicuous advancement of individual people of color served to crystallize a "white backlash," which took many forms – such as anti-busing protests, resistance to affirmative action, and a pattern of more or less coded racist appeals by white politicians, ranging from Reagan's 1980 diatribe against "welfare queens" to Trump's years-long campaign to paint Obama as foreign-born and his obsessive fixation, when he replaced Obama in the White House, on undoing any domestic policy-measure with which Obama could be associated.

Within communities of color, the combined impact of deindustrialization and the drastic reduction of public assistance (welfare payments) made the drug trade financially attractive to people who lacked any other source of income. The long prison terms given to those who were caught up in such activity constituted, in effect, punishment of the poor.[17] The numbers affected by this

---

17 See Loïc Wacquant, "Class, Race, and Hyperincarceration in Revanchist America," in Mumia Abu-Jamal and Johanna Fernández, eds., *The Roots of Mass Incarceration: Locking up Black Dissidents and Punishing the Poor*, special issue of *Socialism and Democracy*, 28:3 (November 2014).

are far greater than the 2+ million people who in the present period are incarcerated at any given moment. Almost all those who have been previously incarcerated suffer long-term disadvantages, including lack of access to many jobs, to many vital services, to loans for college, and to such basic necessities as public housing. State laws block many former prisoners from voting, and new voter-suppression measures have been introduced on a large scale in recent years targeting people on other grounds as well. All these steps taken together have severely cut into the guarantees that were thought to have been achieved as a result of the 1965 Voting Rights Act, which itself, as I noted earlier, was overturned in a 2013 Supreme Court ruling. (The rationale given by the Supreme Court is that there was no longer any need for the federal government to oversee the states' enforcement of voting rights – this, at the very moment when many states were taking new steps precisely to make it more difficult for people to be allowed to vote.)

Policing and prisons

The sheer numbers of people who are incarcerated – approximately 60% of whom are either African American or Latino (more than twice their proportion of the general population) – roughly quintupled between the 1970s and the 2000s. At the same time, there seems also to be an increasing harshness in the way the system's enforcers – police as well as prison guards – treat the populations that are under their watch. While such treatment has never been gentle, new levels of punishment continue to be deployed, in some cases reflecting an ever-growing resort to technological devices. For example, a common practice in Texas prisons is to use toxic gases – even in confined spaces – as well as stun-guns ("tasers"), which are often lethal. In several states, the harshness of prison is increasingly reinforced by the use of video as a substitute for allowing personal visits to prisoners.

The one technological development that has already had some positive effect is the widespread diffusion of smartphones that allow ordinary people to make video recordings of police actions. The circumstances under which police kill someone can now often be ascertained by direct visual evidence, rather than having to be guessed at from the conflicting testimony of police on the one hand and civilian witnesses on the other. This has remarkably enhanced public awareness. It is also argued, in some quarters, that installing video cameras everywhere (including on police uniforms) will exercise a restraining effect on the "enforcers." The full and complete application of such devices appears unreliable, however, and the idea of depending on them follows the typical pattern of pursuing a superficial technological response to a problem – a response whose only guaranteed impact is to create a new "market" – as opposed to addressing the underlying social issues.

In terms of prisons, the excesses of punishment in the US system are quite remarkable. The sheer numbers of people that are locked up reflect in part the extraordinary length of many sentences. Examples include Life Without Possibility of Parole (LWOPP), applied in some cases even to persons under 18; also, the surreal aggregation of multiple sentences, arriving in one case I know of at a total of 241 years – with the convict, who was sentenced at age 16, not becoming eligible for parole until he reaches the age of 112![18] Also noteworthy is the widespread application – affecting about 80,000 prisoners at any one time – of prolonged solitary confinement (recognized by the United Nations as a form of torture), in some cases lasting for decades. This and other punishments within the prison are applied with great arbitrariness, often in reprisal for political activity. In many prisons, provocations and beatings of prisoners by guards are a routine occurrence, along with willful neglect or abuse of prisoners suffering health emergencies.[19] And yet the US government claims moral authority in the international arena on questions of human rights.

---

[18] Owen Amos, "The Teenager Sentenced to 241 Years in Prison," BBC News, March 30, 2018, https://www.bbc.com/news/world-us-canada-43461521

[19] See the reports by Kevin "Rashid" Johnson, http://rashidmod.com/

In terms of the general cultural environment that I've been discussing, it is also relevant to mention some of the smaller vindictive measures, which are significant for the contempt they display for basic human sensibilities. In addition to the practice of replacing personal visits with video hookups, there are also persistent moves – sometimes successfully resisted – toward cutting back the number of days available for visits. All these practices of course vary between states and between prisons of various security levels, but the trends pushed from above, at least for the "high security" prisons, are consistently in the direction of making conditions more painful rather than more redemptive for prisoners. Indiana prisons, for example, do not allow their inmates to receive greeting cards or crayon drawings. Prisons in Virginia and Pennsylvania deliver to their inmates only photocopies and not originals of the letters that are sent to them. The Virginia system requires all visitation applications to be submitted via a central website and does not allow you, unless you are a relative, to be on the visiting list for more than one prisoner. Pennsylvania even tried to forbid book orders to prisoners, but this step was later rescinded in the wake of an ACLU (American Civil Liberties Union) lawsuit.

Much more could be said about the abuse of prisoners and about the lack of interest on the part of the system in seeing those who are released do well for themselves in the outside society. But the core point is that the official ideology of "corrections" is one that promotes a feeling of moral entitlement on the part of guards to view their charges as not deserving of decent treatment. This assumption is the present-day counterpart of the slave-master's sense of the entitlements of ownership. It reflects an attitude that carries over into the impulse to view certain sets of people as no more than targets on which to vent one's anger. There is no room for the idea that every human being, at the deepest level, has needs and desires similar to one's own. The incapacity to recognize this gives free rein to the cruelest impulses (exemplified recently by the policy of separating refugee children from their parents). When such a mindset drives a substantial portion of a society's population, including some at the highest levels of power, it becomes a menace of global proportions.

Lecture 4

CAN THE LEFT BECOME A MAJOR PLAYER IN US POLITICS?

Background

The socialist project is almost as old as capitalism. This reflects the fact that the rapacity and instability of capitalism were evident from its earliest days. Hence the celebrated statement by Marx and Engels, after describing (in the Communist Manifesto) the rise to power of the new class of capitalists, that "a similar movement [of one social order replacing another] is going on before our own eyes" – as the capitalist class was creating its own "gravediggers."

How would the peculiarities of the US affect the way the socialist project evolved in this country?

The socialist movement in the US evolved, as elsewhere, out of labor struggles. These were especially bitter, in the early 20th century, in the factories of the Northeast and in the mining regions of the West. Much of the support for socialism arose from the failure of the early labor organizations – notably, unions of skilled workers grouped in the American Federation of Labor (AFL) – to adequately represent these sectors. The more radical Industrial Workers of the World (IWW) was popular in the West, but was from the outset subject to violent repression. Its most prominent leader, Bill Haywood, was also among the leaders of the Socialist Party.

The Socialist Party of America, founded in 1900, was led by Eugene V. Debs, whose background was as a labor leader in the American Railway Union. With Debs as its regular candidate in presidential elections, the party enjoyed significant growth up to the time of World War I. Its weekly newspaper, the *Appeal to Reason*, had a national circulation of over 700,000 in 1912, the year in which Debs won 6% of the presidential vote, while at the local level, especially in the Midwestern states, the party elected over one hundred mayors.[1]

The party up to that point appeared to be following the rising trajectory of its European counterparts. But it suffered from its inability – and perhaps a reluctance on the part of its members – to organize black workers.[2] Black workers were potentially among the most militant,

---

[1] See John Nichols, *The "S" Word: A Short History of an American Tradition … Socialism*, 2nd ed. (New York: Verso, 2015).

[2] This aspect of the party's history was highlighted in the contemporary writings of Hubert Harrison. Jeffrey B. Perry, ed., *A Hubert Harrison Reader* (Middletown, CT: Wesleyan University Press, 2001).

coming out of a long tradition of slave revolts, and being subjected to exceptionally adverse conditions, but the SP would have had to take a strongly proactive approach, including in many places severe risks, in order to reach out to them.

The party was then also hit with heavy repression, rationalized by the patriotic mobilization leading up to the US entry (in 1917) into World War I. The US Socialist Party, unlike the majorities within the various European SPs, remained firm in opposing its country's participation in the war. The US government used a special law passed in 1918 against espionage as the basis for prosecuting socialists and either jailing them or, if they were immigrants, deporting them. Eugene Debs, notably, was imprisoned under this Act in 1918 for a speech he gave calling on young men to refuse to fight in the war.

Repression has never ceased to be a severe problem for the US Left, belying official pretenses at a commitment to freedom of expression. As always, those pretenses have been facilitated by the fact that much of the repression, in the same tradition as that embodied by vigilantes in the South (e.g., the Ku Klux Klan) and by bounty-hunters killing Indians in the West, has been carried out by non-governmental agents, relying on a general culture of conformity, transmitted by the media and reinforced by community pressure, often stoked by religious preachers.

In any case, although Debs again drew almost a million votes in his 1920 presidential run (which he conducted from prison), repression greatly weakened the Socialist Party, some of whose remaining members split off to form the Communist Party. The CPUSA was from the beginning stigmatized because of its ties to the Soviet Union. Nonetheless, its members for the next two decades constituted the backbone of the US Left. As noted earlier, the CP stressed the importance of organizing across racial lines, and its members had the commitment to run serious risks in order to do so. When the economy sank into depression after 1929, receptivity to the CP showed a dramatic rise.

The CP played a key role in the new step, for the labor movement, of organizing across whole industries ("industrial unionism"), as opposed to the restrictive AFL practice of organizing on the basis of particular craft-skills. This new level of activity led to the formation, in the 1930s, of the more militant CIO (Congress of Industrial Organizations) and, with it, to the reluctant acceptance by the capitalist class of the need to recognize and deal with labor unions.

Along with its labor organizing, the CP promoted radical awareness and sensibility in all domains of life. While economic conditions produced a sense of crisis, the reforms enacted at the federal level, which in part reflected pressure from CP mobilizations, provided further openings for political work. This was especially true of the various educational and cultural projects that were established under the New Deal agenda advanced in the 1930s by President Franklin D. Roosevelt. As the CP was at that time oriented toward collaborating with a wide range of liberal-to-leftwing organizations, it found large audiences for its message. It also drew strength from the successes of the Soviet Union, in those years, in avoiding the economic collapse that befell the capitalist countries and in raising the cultural level of its working class.[3]

The Soviet connection, however, was to prove a double-edged sword. It became a handicap when, during the period of the Soviet Non-Aggression Pact with Nazi Germany (1939-41), it required the CPs around the world to suspend their anti-fascist work, which had been integral to their role in building a broad Left. The Soviet connection again became a handicap following the end of World War II, when the US government, after its temporary wartime alliance with the Soviet Union, returned to its basic stance of global counterrevolution, which we noted earlier. This provided the pretext for the extreme repression that was imposed in the US from about 1946 to 1960.[4]

---

[3] See Michael E. Brown et al., eds., *New Studies in the Politics and Culture of U.S. Communism* (New York: Monthly Review Press, 1993).

[4] See Joel Kovel, *Red Hunting in the Promised Land: Anticommunism in the Making of America* (New York: Basic Books, 1994), and Ellen Schrecker, *Many Are the Crimes: McCarthyism in America* (Boston: Little, Brown, 1998).

That repression or Red Scare, sometimes known as McCarthyism (for the Senator who built his career on denouncing people as communists), was another rather distinctive feature of US political history. Elsewhere, such a drastic campaign of intimidation, which resulted in two executions, scores of jail terms, hundreds of exiles, and thousands of firings, would have required an overthrow of the constitutional regime, or at least some formal declaration of a state of emergency. In the US, by contrast, the whole process was comfortably implemented within the existing framework, which provided enough distractions and enough scope for debate on secondary issues to allow political life to go on as usual – with its narrowly circumscribed debates – as if nothing extraordinary was taking place.

The New Left of the 1960s

The great spur to a revival of the Left, after the postwar repression, came from the civil rights movement to end racial segregation. The other major focus, in terms of mobilizing broad support, was resistance to the US war in Vietnam. Both these issues were tied in part to international developments – in particular, the anti-colonial liberation movements – and both had a major impact on university and college students (partly, in regard to the war, because men under 26 were subject to compulsory military service). In any case, the biggest organization specifically identified with the New Left was an organization of students: Students for a Democratic Society (SDS).

Again, the racial division made itself felt in the movement as a whole, given that SDS, although supportive of the civil rights and Black Power movements (and including in its ranks members who had collaborated directly with these movements), was itself organized at campuses where – as was typical at the time except at Historically Black Colleges and Universities (HBCUs) – students of color constituted a tiny minority. So, while there was solidarity across racial lines, SDS as an organization did not succeed in becoming multiracial. The basic social setting was one that encouraged people of the various ethnicities to organize separately (notably, in addition to the Black organizations, Puerto Ricans in The Young Lords, and Mexican Americans – "Chicanos" – in *La Raza*).

Anchored neither in the labor movement nor in the anti-oppression movements of people of color, the predominantly white student movement was vulnerable to a certain lack of structure. That trait was reinforced by the sense that, following the demise of the CP's influence, it was necessary to develop a new "movement culture," not hampered by notions of party discipline that were associated with the CP's Soviet ties and that required conformity to positions dictated from outside its immediate struggles. Reacting against CP discipline thus tended to translate into rejecting any kind of discipline, a posture that could lead to chaotic national meetings, within which any subgroup that operated in a disciplined fashion could have a disproportionate impact.

Pointing in a similar direction, but with positive as well as negative effects, was a strong emphasis on personal relationships and conduct. Again, this was a kind of reaction to what was viewed as the CP's excessive subordination of the individual to the party. The positive aspect of this reaction was its recognition that social transformation required transformation of the individual as well as of the structures of power. This recognition also aided in the acceptance of demands by oppressed or marginalized sectors for due respect to their members as full participants in the movement. On the negative side, however, the concentration on the personal could also lead to ignoring the need for individuals to sometimes prioritize collective or strategic considerations over their own immediate desires.

The New Left of the 1960s, having been called into existence by urgent ongoing struggles (for racial equality and against an imperialist war), was successful in winning its most immediate demands but not in forging a comprehensive and well defined political force that could challenge the underlying sources of oppression.[5] Nonetheless, its cultural impact was considerable. At least there would now have to be some formal respect

---

5 Victor Wallis, "Keeping the Faith: The U.S. Left, 1968-1998," *Monthly Review*, September 1998.

accorded, in the general culture, to the claims of groups previously marginalized or disrespected on the pretext of either their ethnicity, their gender or sexual orientation, or their age or disability. Only in the context of such respect would it be possible to draw individuals from these groups into any class-based political movement.

Systemic crisis, neoliberalism, and new openings

The movements of the 1960s arose under conditions in which the majority of the US population enjoyed a relatively high – and rising – standard of living. Beginning in the early 1970s, however, a new era began to take shape. The US lost its economic supremacy in the capitalist world (which had reflected its transitory good fortune of not having suffered wartime destruction). Corporations became more global; industrial jobs moved outside the country; and, in reaction to the rising popular movements of the 1960s (the "excess of democracy" bewailed by Professor Huntington), right-wing forces began to launch a counter-offensive. We have noted the War on Drugs as part of this process. More broadly, corporate moguls with huge fortunes established "think tanks" such as the Heritage Foundation, the American Enterprise Institute, and the Cato Institute, and developed plans to completely undo the progressive legacy of the New Deal era (the 1930s).[6]

Ronald Reagan, a rabidly anticommunist movie-actor who had been the Republican Governor of California since 1967, became the standard-bearer for this political project and, under adverse economic conditions (and with the help of secret dealings by his campaign to embarrass the incumbent president – Jimmy Carter – by delaying the release of US hostages in Iran[7]), won the US presidency in the election of 1980. The right-wing ideological shift was so strong that the Democrats were swept along by it, and soon embraced the attack on social welfare that the Republicans had initiated, joining Republican calls for "small government," a deregulated economy, and harsh policies on crime.[8]

The Left, meanwhile, was fragmented. No single hegemonic Left organization emerged from the mobilizations of the 1960s. A relatively small segment turned toward forms of armed struggle. This included

---

[6] See Thomas Ferguson, *Right Turn: The Decline of the Democrats and the Future of American Politics* (New York: Hill & Wang, 1986), and Jane Mayer, *Dark Money: The Hidden History of the Billionaires behind the Rise of the Radical Right* (New York: Doubleday, 2016).

[7] Gary Sick, *October Surprise: America's Hostages in Iran and the Election of Ronald Reagan* (New York: Times Books/Random House, 1991).

[8] This was the agenda of the Democratic Leadership Council, founded in 1984 with the prominent participation of future president Bill Clinton and future vice-president Al Gore.

the Weather Underground, which emerged from a split in SDS, and the Black Liberation Army, whose members sought to respond militarily to police suppression of the Black Panther Party. The Weather Underground bombed targets associated with the US government's war effort, but took care to avoid human casualties of the bombings. The BLA's project, on the other hand, included killing police officers. Neither clandestine movement, however, grew much beyond its initial core. Surviving members of the BLA and its allies have been in prison for decades, with only a few released after extensive campaigns on their behalf.

Outside the clandestine sector, groups anchored in the various oppressed racial/national communities and influenced by the Chinese Revolution turned increasingly to Marxism-Leninism, constituting what became known as the New Communist Movement (NCM). Several of these groups – including from Chicano, African-American, and Asian/Pacific Islander constituencies – merged to form the League of Revolutionary Struggle, which lasted from 1978 to 1990. Although most of the NCM groups broke up after the 1980s – partly because of internal contradictions and partly from external attacks, amplified by repercussions from the fall of the Soviet bloc –, some of their members did political work of lasting importance in certain labor union locals, especially among the United Auto Workers, and in movements for environmental and electoral reform.[9]

For the rest, many of the individuals who had been radicalized during the 1960s continued their work separately, some in single-issue organizations, some in the education sector, and the rest in a variety of occupations. In many cases, it was possible to apply ideas gained in the course of their earlier political experience, in some cases by founding special programs in universities (e.g., Black Studies, Women's Studies), and in others by starting organizations of professionals with a political agenda (e.g., Science for the People; Physicians for a National Health Program).

Overall, radical activity was to some degree kept alive, through the 1980s and '90s, by the continuing efforts of identity-groupings that emerged from the "new social movements" associated with the 1960s Left. An exceptionally effective example was the Gay Rights movement, a sector of which responded to the health emergency arising from the AIDS epidemic of the mid-1980s with disruptive actions that compelled a positive political response. Although Gay Rights, as such, was not an anti-capitalist movement, its initial energy owed much to the 1960s Left. Removal of the social stigma that

---

[9] For insight on the NCM, I am grateful to Eric Mann of the Labor/Community Strategy Center. See also Max Elbaum, *Revolution in the Air: Sixties Radicals Turn to Lenin, Mao and Che* (New York: Verso, 2002).

previously surrounded homosexuality can be considered a positive step, although one that – like the earlier emergence of labor unions and the new openings for black politicians – did not by itself weaken class rule.

An electoral alternative?

The repudiation by leading Democrats of their party's progressive tradition created political space for a Left alternative, but structural factors have made it difficult for a Left party to get any significant number of votes. The repressive steps of the early 20th century had also included many states setting very strict requirements – unlike those of other constitutional regimes – for any party other than the two dominant ones to be assigned a place on the ballot.[10] Voters thus remain under enormous pressure to limit their choices to one of the two "acceptable" alternatives. Under these conditions, Democrats have come to be viewed by progressive voters as a "lesser evil," and we must constantly refer to a "lesser evil" dynamic in US elections – although how much less of an evil the Democrats are (in their core priorities) remains an open question.[11]

---

10 The uniquely repressive nature of the US electoral system is highlighted in Seth Ackerman, "A Blueprint for a New Party," *Jacobin* [online], 2016.

11 See Victor Wallis, "'Lesser Evil' as Argument and Tactic, from Marx to the Present," in Marcello Musto, ed., *Marx for Today* (London: Routledge, 2012).

In 1980, progressive activists organized the Citizens Party to support a run for president by the well-known environmental scientist Barry Commoner. Commoner was a frequent commentator on mainstream media before he became a presidential candidate, but as soon as his candidacy was announced, the media completely blacked him out, and he received an insignificant number of votes. In 1984 and 1988, much of the Left was drawn into the effort by Rev. Jesse Jackson, with his background in the civil rights movement, to become (as a Democrat) the first African American major-party nominee for US president. An eloquent speaker, Jackson challenged the right-wing turn of top Democrats. His progressive populist message resonated across racial lines, as he championed the cause of workers even in all-white constituencies. He revived the idea of the Rainbow Coalition that had been pioneered within a revolutionary perspective by Fred Hampton; however, despite his dissident stance relative to other Democratic candidates, Jackson had no interest in promoting an independent force, and when his 1988 campaign was over, he simply disbanded the Coalition – even as an organization within the party.

In the 1990s, Left attempts at breaking up the Democrat/Republican "duopoly" took three forms.

One approach, possible only in states that permitted more than one party to endorse a particular electoral candidate, was a practice known as "fusion" (fusing two parties behind a single candidate). The idea, put forward by a group calling itself the New Party, was that if the Democrats presented a candidate who had at least a somewhat progressive record, then the New Party, rather than run a candidate of its own (thereby splitting the progressive vote), would co-endorse the Democrats' candidate, and would urge people to vote for that candidate on the New Party ballot-line rather than on the official (Democrat) line, so that the candidate would feel accountable to the more progressive views of the New Party's base. But only one state (New York) had an electoral law that permitted this practice of co-endorsement, and efforts to extend it to other states were unsuccessful.

A more important initiative was the attempt to form a Labor Party (LP), which would be built up on the basis of support from labor unions. The leadership of the labor movement had always supported the Democrats, but there was much discontent with the Democrats among union members. The LP strategy was based on the recognition that it would be impossible to directly challenge the Democrats without first building up a strong organizational base, which it proposed to do within the union movement, before presenting its own candidates in any election. However, the notion of a political party was so strongly linked, in US practice, to the purely electoral function of parties, that the LP's failure to run candidates in elections prevented it from generating wide interest.

The third approach was that of the Greens or Green Party, which since the mid-1980s had been running their own candidates in local elections, and which, starting in 1996, has also run presidential candidates. The Greens have had some victories at the local level, especially in elections to city councils that are not organized along party lines. They have only rarely elected representatives to state legislatures. At the national level, they generated significant support in the 2000 election for their presidential candidate Ralph Nader,[12] a lawyer who since late 1950s had been a well-known and highly respected advocate for consumers against fraudulent and sometimes dangerous practices of private corporations. Nader's exposés of corporate crime were so popular that although his campaign was almost completely blacked out by the mass media, he nonetheless was favored by 10-12 percent of the population, according to surveys.

What ultimately prevented Nader from having a real chance in the election was the fact that the nationally televised debates between presidential candidates are administered by a committee composed exclusively of Democrats and Republicans (in equal numbers). Both these dominant parties felt threatened by the issues and the arguments that Nader was raising, and they had the authority to prevent him from appearing in the debates. With Nader excluded, many potential voters who were attracted by his program ceased to view him as a viable

---

[12] Nader ran on the Green ticket but did not join the Green Party.

candidate, and he ended up receiving only about 3% of the national vote. More recent Green candidacies have drawn even less. Against two exceptionally unpopular dominant-party candidates in 2016, Green Party nominee Jill Stein – a medical doctor with essentially socialist convictions and with excellent debating skills – received only about 1% of the vote.

The obstacles to running a left-wing presidential campaign are enormous. We shall consider these further in the next lecture, when we look at the 2016 attempt to implement such a project within the framework of the Democratic Party. Given all these obstacles, there is considerable skepticism on the Left as to the value of electoral work. Elections even come to be seen, under these conditions, as drawing the energy of activists away from the vital task of directly affecting policy. It is often noted in this connection that the most progressive legislation since the 1960s – all the current laws protecting the environment – was enacted during the Republican presidency of Richard Nixon: not thanks to his initiative, but thanks to the existence of strong popular movements.

As there is so little chance of electing to office anyone with strong Left positions, the electoral struggle reverts to being defined as building up support for "lesser evil" candidates, who often end up, if they win, pursuing policies that are just as bad as those of the candidates that they defeated. The example of the election of 2004 comes to mind. Hundreds of thousands of people had demonstrated in 2003 against President Bush Jr.'s planned invasion of Iraq. However, instead of amplifying even further this expression of opposition, much of the energy of those opposed to Bush's policies was diverted to supporting the electoral challenge to Bush by the Democrats. But the Democrats' chosen candidate, Senator John Kerry, although running against Bush, did not dissent from Bush's war policy. The election thus had the effect of largely silencing public opposition to the war.

Many other examples of this effect could be cited. The question remains of how the Left can use elections for political education purposes without letting such electoral work absorb all of its limited resources. Until elections offer the real possibility of victory to a party with a radical program, they serve as a mechanism for creating a false impression that the government is accountable to the people.

Popular movements since the 1990s

Because of the adverse effects of neoliberal policies, and because of increasing alarm about the environmental crisis, grassroots opposition movements continued to grow throughout the 1990s, in tandem with parallel movements in other countries. This process culminated in November/December 1999 with the massive civil-disobedience demonstrations in Seattle against the founding conference of the World Trade Organization.

The demonstrations were impressive not only for their scale (thousands willing to risk arrest for civil disobedience), but also for the breadth of the organizations involved, spanning several continents and including labor unions as well as environmentalists ("Teamsters and Turtles"). This looked to be the beginning of a new level of struggle, regularly targeting major ruling-class gatherings around the world.

The process suffered a severe setback, however, in the aftermath of the September 11 (9/11) attacks in 2001. Almost immediately after those attacks, a wide-ranging law was passed, with almost no debate, by the US Congress, called the USA Patriot Act. Its alleged purpose was to defend the country against terrorism, but it defined the punishable offenses so loosely and vaguely that they could be extended to apply to any acts of resistance – including nonviolent ones – against the policies or physical gatherings of the ruling class. In subsequent years, for example, nonviolent demonstrators at the presidential nominating conventions of the Republicans and Democrats would be preventively detained *en masse*, and some of their organizers would be prosecuted on charges of terrorism. (Terrorism charges would also be filed against ecological activists when their disclosures were thought to threaten the profits of targeted companies.)

But capitalist practice continued to generate widespread opposition. In 2008 there was a major financial crisis which led to millions of people in the US losing their jobs and/or their homes. This eventually inspired (in late 2011) the "Occupy Wall Street" movement, which, during the brief time it was allowed to continue – with its largely spontaneous encampments in many cities –, introduced a lasting new phrase into US political discourse: "the 1 percent versus the 99 percent." By 2012, a survey showed that among people under the age of 30, despite generations of capitalist indoctrination, there was more support for socialism than for capitalism.

It's hard to predict what opportunities will arise to bring significant advances in the revolutionary process. We still lack a cohesive mass political force of the Left. But opportunities to raise the level of awareness are constantly presenting themselves. The widely publicized killings mostly of black people by police officers in 2014 precipitated a massive outpouring of protest under the slogan "Black Lives Matter." Instances of sexual assault and cases of mass shootings likewise offer opportunities for impassioned debate as to what may be the underlying causes of such repeated expressions of aggressive impulses. And one of the immediate reactions to Donald Trump's accession to the presidency, apart from nationwide demonstrations targeting his disrespect of women, was a sudden five-fold increase in membership of Democratic Socialists of America – a social-democratic organization founded in 1981 whose electoral work is within the orbit of the Democratic Party but whose mostly young new members are calling that affiliation into question.

Meanwhile, mass incarceration may also have its payback effect on those who preside over it. Sites of extreme oppression are cauldrons for the awakening of consciousness. In 2013, there was an effective hunger strike in the California prisons – unified across racial lines – against the barbaric practice of prolonged solitary confinement. And in 2017, there was the beginning of a national movement against prison slavery. By the following year, this had grown into a strike movement that raised a full range of demands aimed at restoring prisoners' civil and human rights.[13] The resulting growth in public awareness was surely a factor in the 2018 Florida referendum in which, with 65 percent popular approval, some 1.5 million persons who had been disenfranchised because of felony convictions recovered their right to vote.

George Jackson, the revolutionary writer/activist assassinated by California guards in 1971, expressed the idea that if prison doesn't destroy you, it makes you indestructible – or at least gives you an unshakeable sense of the need for struggle.[14] The leaders of the prison movements – and many of their participants – are well educated in revolutionary thinking that was not offered to them in school. They could play an important role in any wider movement.

---

13 See https://incarceratedworkers.org/

14 "This camp brings out the very best in brothers or destroys them entirely." *Soledad Brother: The Prison Letters of George Jackson* (New York: Bantam Books, 1970), 32.

Lecture 5
THE CURRENT US POLITICAL SCENE

Capitalism unhinged
I consider the current US political scene to be one in which capitalism has become totally unhinged. By this I mean that the capitalist ruling class has aggressively rejected every possible restraint upon its freedom of action. It has brought to power a government that not only promotes capitalist interests, but is committed to dismantling all previous steps taken to limit the damage arising from capitalist practice, such as speculative excesses, economic insecurity (for working-class people), and harm to the environment.

It is no accident that the government that embodies this agenda is one whose top leader stands to profit personally from the policies that are being implemented. Equally consistent with this agenda are the expressions of racism, misogyny, and xenophobia coming from the highest levels and extending their poison throughout the society – in the form of violent demonstrations, racist killings by police, mass shootings by individuals, beatings by prison guards, acts of gratuitous cruelty to refugee families (separating children from their parents), and assaults on the reproductive rights of women (de-funding health services and forbidding federally funded healthcare providers from even mentioning the word "abortion").

The background to this complex of behaviors is partly apparent from historical practices that we have already discussed, in particular, the genocidal assault on the indigenous population, the institution of slavery, and the enforcement structures and cultural apparatus that evolved to sustain those practices. What I want to underline here, however, is the point that all these practices arose directly out of the economic drive to expansion. The reason such practices are less extreme in other capitalist countries is that in those countries the capitalist drive has been to some degree offset and restrained by political forces expressive of working-class or popular interests (forces that in the US were decisively weakened by the racial divide). What the US displays is the mix of ultra-aggressive behaviors that can develop in a population when class interests opposed to those of capital have not been able to constitute an effective (civilizing) political force.

The struggle against such behaviors is obviously a continuing one, as the lack of accountability to which they lead – at the highest levels – is clearly unacceptable to a majority of the population (which consistently favors progressive reforms such as universal healthcare, environmental protection, quality public education, and taxing the rich). We shall examine some of the specific ways in which the contending social forces interact, but we first need to ask how the current extreme situation came into being.

An interval of hope (the 1930s)

The present period is not the first one in which capitalism has been unhinged. That happened also earlier, in the period leading up to the economic collapse of 1929. The differences between the present period and that earlier one reflect the political developments of the intervening decades, on top of the cumulative toll taken on the ecological infrastructure, which has now reached a breaking point in several dimensions.[1] Ruling-class resistance to progressive or regulatory reform has in recent years become more intransigent than it was in the earlier period, and has been buttressed, especially in certain sectors of the white male population, by the effects of permanent imperialist war and the associated cultural conditioning.[2]

---

1 See Fred Magdoff and John Bellamy Foster, *What Every Environmentalist Needs to Know about Capitalism* (New York: Monthly Review Press, 2011).
2 "How America's Perpetual Warfare Abroad Is Fueling an Increase in White Supremacist Violence in U.S.," https://www.democracynow.org/2018/11/20/

The New Deal of the 1930s remains the period of the most progressive social policies in US history. These included the important idea that when capitalist enterprises could not employ workers, then the government had a responsibility to create jobs directly in public enterprises or public services. The availability of jobs in the public sector naturally put the working class in a stronger position to resist the conditions that would be imposed upon them by the private (capitalist) sector. For this reason, a faction of the capitalist class vehemently opposed this policy. President Roosevelt, for his part, said that he welcomed this faction's hatred of him. But a more far-sighted group within the capitalist class supported Roosevelt's approach. Its members recognized that, with unemployment having reached 25% of the labor force, there was a real danger of working-class revolt. As one of Roosevelt's capitalist advisers later remarked, "in those days I felt and said I would be willing to part with half of what I had if I could be sure of keeping, under law and order, the other half."[3]

Despite the New Deal's basic agenda of saving capitalism, its public works programs, especially the Works Progress Administration (WPA), pressed by a wave of militant labor organizing in 1934, created numerous opportunities – in the form of commissioned

---

3 Joseph P. Kennedy (patriarch of the Kennedy dynasty), quoted in G. William Domhoff, *Who Rules America?* 1st ed. (Englewood Cliffs, NJ: Prentice-Hall, 1967), 153.

public art works, theatrical projects, etc. – for political education inspired by socialist visions. On the other hand, however, the government never had any intent to nationalize profit-making activities. Moreover, despite the New Deal's success in relieving some of the Depression-era misery, the capitalist recovery was incomplete, and there was another increase in unemployment (in the late 1930s) that ended only with the militarization of the economy accompanying US entry into World War II.

The New Deal's progressive agenda was also compromised by race-based restrictions on its benefits. This was the period when the apartheid Jim Crow system still governed the Southern states, whose uniformly racist congressional representatives played a decisive role in limiting the scope of social legislation at the national level. As a result, the Social Security Act excluded agricultural and domestic workers, 60 percent of whom were black. Poor black women moreover were in practice largely excluded from widows' benefits. Meanwhile, as if to underscore the thrust of such restrictions, Roosevelt refused to press for a federal anti-lynching law.[4]

---

4 See Ira Katznelson, *Fear Itself: The New Deal and the Origins of Our Time* (New York: Liveright, 2013), Part II.

Stages of repression

A decisive step toward reversing the New Deal's progressive direction was taken in 1944. The vice-president during Roosevelt's third 4-year term (which had begun in 1941) was an agrarian populist named Henry A. Wallace who had strong progressive values. Although Roosevelt's health was poor at the time, there was general agreement in the Democratic Party that he should seek re-election to a fourth term (it was not until some years later that the presidency was limited to two terms). But it was also understood that Roosevelt would likely not live long enough to serve out the full term. The choice of vice-president thus became crucial, and the conservative leaders of the party forced Wallace out, replacing him with Senator Harry S. Truman, who in 1941, before US entry into World War II, had expressed publicly the hope that the forces of Nazi Germany and the Soviet Union would destroy each other.

It was Truman, of course, who in August 1945 (less than four months after Roosevelt's death) would order the atomic bombing of Japan. It was widely understood, at the level of top US leadership, that this bombing was militarily unnecessary to securing Japanese surrender. Subsequent historical research showed that the decision to use the bomb was based on the goal of gaining geopolitical advantage over the Soviet Union in East

Asia.[5] It was also Truman (like Roosevelt, a Democrat), who, as we have noted, articulated the post-war US mission of global counterrevolutionary intervention. A key figure in this process was Allen Dulles, a corporate lawyer who embodied the close links between the private and the public sector on which US capitalism has depended. Dulles played a central role in 1) recruiting Nazi officers (after their defeat) into the US Intelligence apparatus, 2) founding the Central Intelligence Agency (CIA) (established under Truman's orders in 1947) and, in particular, the CIA's Covert Operations division, and 3) (later) laying the groundwork for the assassination of President Kennedy and then, as self-appointed mastermind of the Warren Commission, guiding the official cover-up.[6]

The general climate of repression that prevailed throughout the 1950s, as we have seen, helped shape the conditions under which the eruption of popular protest would evolve. The radical drive of the 1960s was strong enough to bring new progressive measures, including not only the Voting Rights Act and the environmental protection laws, but also the introduction of Food Stamps as a program to provide relief to the poor. But

---

[5] Gar Alperovitz, *Atomic Diplomacy: Hiroshima and Potsdam*, 2nd ed. (London: Pluto Press, 1994).

[6] David Talbot, *The Devil's Chessboard: Allen Dulles, the CIA, and the Rise of America's Secret Government* (New York: HarperCollins, 2015).

violence persisted on the part of government agencies and vigilantes – from racists killing civil rights activists to National Guard troops killing student demonstrators to federal and local police forces decimating the leadership of the Black Panther Party. As popular protest continued to grow – culminating in rebellious actions by US soldiers against their commanding officers in Vietnam – and as US resources became overstretched by the combined demands of military intervention and social programs, the stage was set for the conservative reaction of the 1970s.

In addition to the War on Drugs, the Reagan presidency (1981-89) brought an abrupt escalation in what has been called "class struggle from above." When the union of Professional Air Traffic Controllers (PATCO) – government employees who ironically had supported Reagan in his campaign – threatened in 1981 to strike for better working conditions, Reagan fired all of them on the spot. This was just his first step. Under his watch, the Labor Department and the National Labor Relations Board became bastions of union-busting.[7] A symbolic expression of Reagan's contempt for progressive values was his order to remove the solar panels which his presidential predecessor Jimmy Carter had installed on the White House roof.

---

[7] Dick Meister, "Ronald Reagan's War on Labor," http://www.dickmeister.com/id89.html

Repression against foreign targets continued with Reagan's invasion of Grenada (1983), Bush Sr.'s attack on Panama (1989), and Bill Clinton's occupation of Haiti (1994) and bombing of Serbia (1999). The drive to suppress the Cuban Revolution was continuous, marked in 1996 by the Helms-Burton Act, which sought to close US ports to ships used for trade with Cuba. The War on Terror, officially proclaimed in 2001, would create the conditions for its own perpetuation.

How to maintain an unpopular agenda

With perpetual US military engagements in many parts of the Muslim world, as well as various forms of CIA intervention elsewhere, not to mention the continuing military presence in Korea and in the South China Sea, the US ruling class needs to maintain a political atmosphere at home in which there are constant reminders of dangers – both real and imaginary – posed to the American people. In the background is the legislative machinery provided by the USA Patriot Act of 2001, which makes it possible to criminalize protest-actions that may be carried out against US foreign policy.

Within this framework, there is routine surveillance of Islamic communities in the US, and, from time to time, there are instances in which undercover FBI agents seek to entrap radical Muslims so that they can be convicted of planning acts of terrorism. (One relevant episode that has still been insufficiently investigated is the bombing that was carried out in 2013 during the Boston Marathon, in relation to which it is known that the FBI had long been tracking the key perpetrator but had not tried to block his re-entry to the US after his trips to his homeland of Chechnya.)

In terms of laws imposed to quell protest, another example is the attempts in several states to punish individuals who advocate Boycott, Divestment and Sanctions ("BDS") against Israel in protest of its policies toward the Palestinians. And I mentioned earlier the federal law against "eco-terrorism," which is significant not because it punishes violent acts – for which laws already exist – but because it also punishes *speech*, when such speech, involving disclosures about a company's inhumane practices, is viewed by the company as threatening its profits.

But the most comprehensive and continuously applied machinery to block a potential progressive upsurge is that which is applied by state governments, political parties, and mass media to the electoral process. We have already noted a key component of this machinery, namely, the many practices that are used to impede the electoral participation of poor people, especially people of color. This, along with ballot-restrictions and media-blackouts affecting anti-capitalist contenders, is the most important ongoing form of control, and although the devices it involves are not used in all of the states, it can have a major impact in presidential contests even if it is implemented in only a few states. Voter-suppression of this sort has taken on increasing importance in recent years, especially through the operations of the American Legislative Exchange Council (ALEC), a private organization which brings together corporate executives and state legislators to advance an aggressive right-wing agenda. The contempt shown for ordinary ethical standards is often shocking, as when electoral processes in particular states are administered by one of the contending candidates.[8]

The whole story of the manipulation of electoral outcomes is a long one, but two elections – those of 2000 and 2016 – deserve particular attention. These are the two most recent instances in which a Republican president has gained a victory after two terms in which the presidency was held by a Democrat (Clinton, 1993-2001; Obama, 2009-17). They are also the two recent cases in which the winning candidate had a smaller national total of votes than the losing candidate.

The election of 2000 centered on the contest between the Republican George W. Bush (Bush Jr.) and the Democrat (then vice-president) Al Gore. The Green Party candidate Ralph Nader, as we have seen, was excluded from the presidential debates and therefore had

---

[8] Georgia's 2018 election for governor was administered by Republican candidate Brian Kemp, who had more than 340,000 registered voters removed from the rolls on the false pretext that they had moved. See https://truthout.org/articles/georgias-kemp-purged-340134-voters-falsely-asserting-they-had-moved/

no chance of getting a large number of votes. The Democrats subsequently tried to blame the Nader candidacy for causing Bush's victory, thinking that they had some kind of inherent entitlement to the support of those who voted for Nader, whereas in fact much of Nader's support came from people who otherwise would not have voted, and some of it came from people who, in classic fashion, would have voted Republican *not* because they accepted the Republican agenda, but rather because they had no other electoral channel by which to express their discontent after two terms of a Democratic presidency.

In fact, the 2000 election was directly stolen by the Republicans, in the most literal sense. Given the final outcomes in all the other states, the victory would go to whichever candidate won the state of Florida. What, then, transpired in Florida?[9] 1) The Florida Secretary of State who administered the election (Katherine Harris) was appointed to that position by Florida Governor Jeb Bush (brother of Bush Jr.), and was the same person who

---

9 This summary of the electoral process is based on Greg Palast's reporting at the time, which no US newspaper would publish (it appeared in the British press). On the Supreme Court's role, see Vincent Bugliosi, *The Betrayal of America: How the Supreme Court Undermined the Constitution and Chose Our President* (New York: Nation Books, 2001). See also Carol Anderson, *One Person, No Vote: How Voter Suppression Is Destroying Our Democracy* (New York: Bloomsbury, 2018).

chaired the state Republican Party committee. 2) For months before the election, under Harris's orders, many residents of black neighborhoods had had their voter-registration status voided on spurious grounds. 3) On the day of the election, the police harassed black citizens driving to the polls and prevented many of them from voting. 4) Although exit polls showed Gore leading, the right-wing TV network Fox News announced prematurely that Bush had won Florida and thereby the presidency. 5) With the apparent difference in vote-totals very small, a recount was ordered, but crowds of Republican operatives sought to block the recount by intimidating election-workers. 6) After a local judge ordered that the recount proceed, and with indications that it would swing the election to Gore, the Republican Party appealed that ruling to the US Supreme Court. 7) The US Supreme Court, in a 5-4 decision, overruled the Florida judge, ordered the recount halted, and awarded the presidency to Bush. The Court based its ruling only on the "harm" that would otherwise be suffered by Bush, completely ignoring any considerations of electoral integrity – or harm to the voters.

Of course, we can only speculate as to how a Gore presidency would have turned out. On the one hand, it has to be acknowledged that his priorities did not differ from those of Bush in any fundamental sense. But on the other hand, we do know that Bush's team had a definite agenda – that of the Project for the New American Century – that included finding some pretext to bring "regime change" to Iraq. Beyond this, the theft of the election is significant in a more general sense, as a reflection of the contempt in which ruling-class politicians hold the principles of democratic accountability. It is noteworthy, in this regard, that when the formal certification of the election outcome came before Congress, Gore, presiding over the process by virtue of his status as vice-president, chose not to challenge it.

As for the 2016 election, its particular interest for us lies in the contest within the Democratic Party (DP) as to who its presidential candidate would be. For the first time, a politician who described himself as a socialist was a serious contender for the DP nomination. Bernie Sanders, a Senator who had not previously joined the DP (and who still calls himself an Independent), had policy positions similar to those of Ralph Nader. But unlike Nader (who had run in 2000 as a Green), he entered the contest within the DP because he recognized that this was the only way he could expect to get at least a modicum of coverage in the corporate media.

Sanders was the only major challenger, within the DP, to Hillary Clinton, who as the former "first lady" (under Bill Clinton) and subsequently, in turn, a Senator, then (in 2008) a candidate for the DP presidential nomination, and then, after losing to Obama, becoming his Secretary of State, was from the beginning the choice of the party leadership. But Hillary Clinton was completely identified with the policies of the previous eight years, which, after the great hope for "change" that attended Obama's 2008 victory, had proved to be disappointing to the party's popular base. She sought to repair her image by, for example, saying that her 2002 Senate vote to authorize invading Iraq was a "mistake" and, later, by switching from supporting to opposing the Trans-Pacific Partnership (TPP) (a "free trade" agreement that would empower an international body of corporate agents to override national laws). But she then named as her vice-presidential running-mate a Senator who supported the TPP. She also claimed to oppose the power of Wall Street despite having been paid large sums by Wall Street bankers for speeches whose content she refused to disclose.

Sanders, significantly, ran a campaign in which he refused to accept contributions from corporations or from corporate Political Action Committees (PACs). He raised substantial sums of money through millions of small donations, averaging $27. Most importantly, he made economic inequality the central issue of his campaign, and he had the oratorical skill to formulate his critique in a way that appealed to working-class people across party lines. It should be kept in mind that although Republican economic policies make no concessions to interests other than those of capital, the party nonetheless appeals to a sector of working-class voters through the conservative and in some cases bigoted positions its politicians take on certain social issues, such as religion, race, immigration, women's rights, and gay rights.

Sanders articulated a progressive stance on all these issues. Although he did not call for an end to capitalism and imperialism, he was nonetheless regarded, both by the DP Establishment and by the corporate media, as someone who was too radical and who would have to be blocked. His speeches received little media coverage, compared to the enormous attention that was given to the exchanges of insults among the various Republican contenders and, in one case, to speculation as to whether or not Trump would appear at a particular event. The DP establishment minimized Sanders' exposure to the public by scheduling the smallest possible number of debates between him and Clinton, and also by having them take place at times when the potential audience would be diverted away from them by major sports events. In addition, Clinton obtained advance information as to the questions that would be posed to the candidates during the debates. There were also electoral irregularities in some of the states, and, further skewing the outcome, a significant number of delegates to the eventual nominating convention ("super-delegates"), who had prior commitments to Clinton, were chosen (based on party rules) in advance of any popular votes.

On the Republican side, Trump's practice is well known. He displayed without apology his misogyny, racism, xenophobia, and general arrogance. But he also sought to paint himself as a "man of the people," and even, absurd as it might seem (especially in light of the appointments he would later make to key policy-making positions), lashed out against "Wall Street."[10] Both he and Clinton, according to surveys, were unpopular with a majority of potential voters. But he had the advantage of being seen as representing a possible "change." The DP leadership, by blocking Sanders, made it possible for Trump to get away with this pretense. Yet all surveys showed that, had the election pitted Sanders against Trump, Sanders would have been the preferred candidate. Indeed, significant numbers of working-class people who had voted for Sanders in the DP primary voted for Trump in the general election.[11]

But the final outcome reflected not only Clinton's shortcomings as a candidate. It also reflected voter-suppression in "swing states" that Trump won by a narrow margin.[12] In Wisconsin, where the winning margin was about 30,000 votes, more than 200,000 people (mostly low-income and therefore likely DP voters) had been disqualified by a new voter-ID law; in Michigan, where the winning margin was only 10,000 votes, some 75,000 in the heavily African-American city

---

10 See my November 2015 column, "The Trump Phenomenon," https://mronline.org/2015/11/25/wallis251115-html/

11 This is dramatically shown in Michael Moore's 2018 film, *Fahrenheit 11/9*.

12 See Palast, *The Best Democracy Money Can Buy* (book and dvd).

of Detroit were lost as a result of malfunctioning optical scanners; in North Carolina, tens of thousands of African-American votes were blocked by a reduction in the number of polling stations. Had Clinton won those three states, she would have defeated Trump.

Where next?

Many people on the US Left see the extreme nature of the Trump presidency as offering a "wake-up call" or a "teaching moment." Will we be able to use this situation to advance people's understanding of the bankruptcy of capitalism?

Senator Sanders, after conceding to Hillary Clinton and throwing his support to her campaign against Trump, established a new organization to promote the agenda he had put forward during his own campaign; he named it "Our Revolution" (OR).

The key medium-term question is how to create a political force of the Left that can be a serious contender for power. This will depend significantly on how any project that can generate major popular commitment relates to the Democratic Party. So far, OR has concentrated on supporting particular DP candidates who proclaim progressive or liberal values. It has not given any indication of wanting to promote a breakaway on the part of such candidates and their supporters from the corporate-dominated DP leadership.

A particular indication of Sanders' reluctance to contemplate calling for a break from the DP is his unwillingness to question the dominant consensus on the US role in the world. His founding statement to OR and his speeches to that organization in the ensuing months contained not a word about US foreign policy. This is important, because the US global role is the one issue that top Democrats and Republicans alike refuse to challenge.[13]

Sanders later spelled out his foreign policy views in a 2017 speech in Fulton, Missouri, in the same venue where British Prime Minister Winston Churchill in 1946 had given the "Iron Curtain" speech that inspired subsequent Cold War rhetoric against the Soviet Union.[14] Sanders criticizes particular instances of US intervention, such as the overthrow of elected governments in Iran (1953) and Chile (1973), and reminds us of his opposition (in 2002) to authorizing the US invasion of Iraq. But his invocation of democracy as a foreign-policy goal is clearly in the Cold War tradition of calling for US global leadership, as exemplified in his fulsome praise of the post-World War II Marshall Plan.[15] And he echoes

---

13 See Laurence H. Shoup, *Wall Street's Think Tank: The Council on Foreign Relations and the Empire of Neoliberal Geopolitics, 1976-2014* (New York: Monthly Review Press, 2015).

14 Video of Sanders' speech: https://www.youtube.com/watch?v=kxvP6jDtt4c

15 The European Recovery Program, advanced by George C. Marshall (Truman's Secretary of State), was integral to the global

the DP's attempt to explain away its 2016 electoral failure by blaming Russian intervention, thereby burying any possible class-based critique of the DP leadership and instead issuing a patriotic call for unity against the supposed "common enemy."[16]

In fact, as we have seen, the Democrats lost partly because of voter-suppression and partly because of their failure to meet the expectations of progressive change aroused by Obama's 2008 campaign. Because of the precarious economic conditions affecting a majority of the US population, the DP is obligated to display – with the current help of Sanders and his OR movement – some empathy for the resulting needs. But the question is whether this response will empower that majority to organize on its own behalf and with a full analysis of the systemic nature of its problems. Is the goal to actually strip the ruling class of its power, or is it merely to extract a few concessions which, like those given in the 1930s or like the 1965 Voting Rights Act, will later be taken back?

---

interventionist agenda that we examined in Lecture 2. On the Cold War logic of the ERP or Marshall Plan, see Frank Kofsky, *Harry S. Truman and the War Scare of 1948* (New York: St. Martin's Press, 1993), esp. Chapter 5. On the general US prioritization of capitalism over democracy in postwar Europe, see Talbot, *The Devil's Chessboard*, and William Blum, *Killing Hope: U.S. Military and CIA Interventions Since World War II* (Monroe, ME: Common Courage Press, 2003).

16 On "Russiagate," see above, Lecture 2, footnote 10.

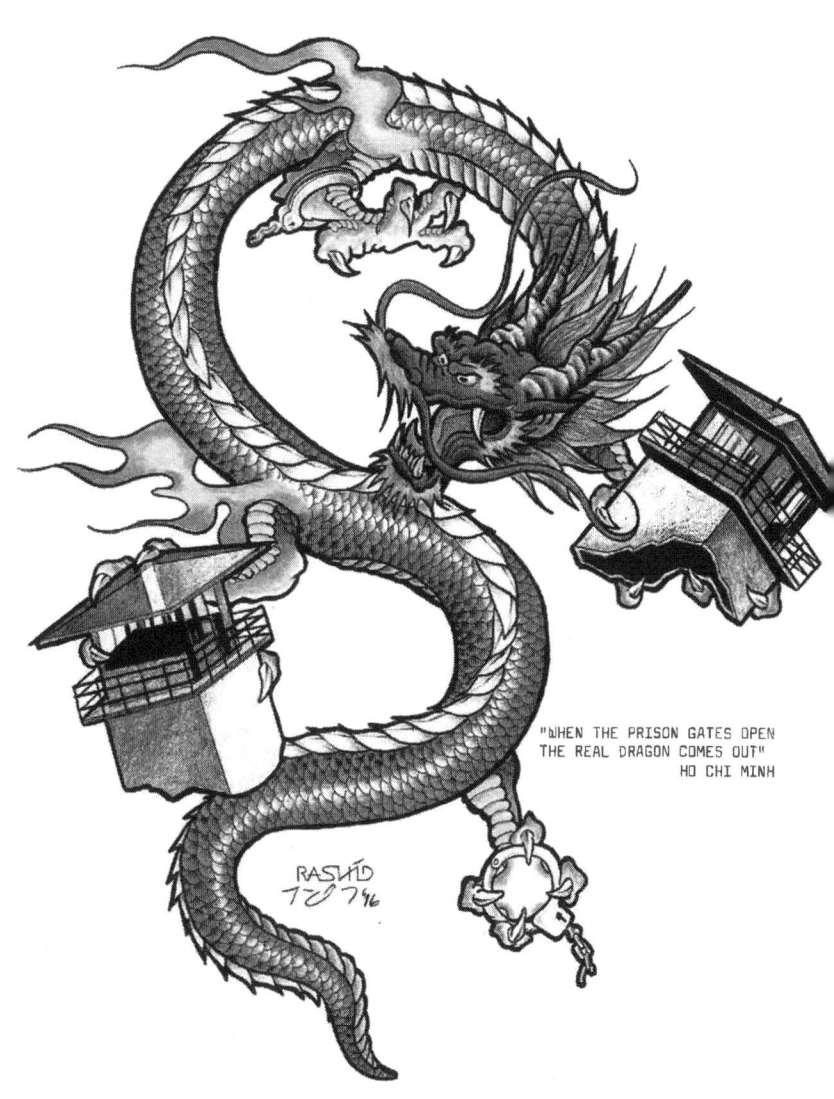

Because of the environmental crisis, time is short for making the necessary changes. If the only changes that are made stay within the limits of what is acceptable to the capitalist ruling class, relief from current hardships and dangers will be minimal. The current logic of the US political system – of a regular alternation in office between two factions of the ruling class – has already for much too long blocked popular recognition of the need for a radical power-shift. The Left cannot ignore the discussions taking place within the DP, but it also has to avoid being sucked into them. It must consistently pose a superior alternative[17] and must provide a pole of attraction to people for when they finally come to see – with its help – that the reigning duopoly is like a "good cop/bad cop" performance in which the bad cop has the last word.

---

17 This is the task to which my book, *Red-Green Revolution: The Politics and Technology of Ecosocialism* (Toronto and Chicago: Political Animal Press, 2018), seeks to contribute.

INDEX

abortion, 92
advertising
    for political campaigns, 11
    media dependence on, 18
Afghanistan, 23
    US invasion of, 43
    women and US role, 34f
Africa,
    European massacres in, 26
    US intervention in, 22
AIDS epidemic, 80
American Civil Liberties Union, 67
American Enterprise Institute, 77
American Federation of Labor (AFL), 70, 72
American Legislative Exchange Council (ALEC), 102
anti-colonial liberation movements, 74
armed self-defense, 55, 56
armed struggle, 78f
assassinations, 58-60, 97

bin Laden, Osama, 43n
Black Codes, 50
Black Liberation Army, 79
"Black Lives Matter," 88
Black Panther Party (BPP)
    founding of, 56
    impact, 60
    suppression of, 79, 98
Black Power, 56, 75
Black Studies programs, 80
Blum, William
    Killing Hope, 40
Boston Marathon bombing, 101
Boycott, Divestment, Sanctions (BDS), 101
Burchett, Wilfred, 36
Bush Jr. (George W.), 32, 37, 43, 44n, 86
    in 2000 election, 102-104
Bush Sr. (George H.W.), 43, 100
Bush, Jeb, 103

California

prisoners fighting forest fires, 50n
2013 prison hunger strike, 89, 90
capital punishment, 27
capitalism, 69, 107, 109
capitalist interests, 10, 13, 17
  as basis for racism and imperialism, 47f
  conflated by media with democracy, 32f
  unrestrained expression of, 91f
Carter, Jimmy, 78, 98
Cato Institute, 77
census
  counting of prisoners, 16
Central Intelligence Agency (CIA)
  covert operations, 22
  founding of, 97
  interventions, 100
children, rights of, 4
Chile
  overthrow of elected government, 41f, 110
China, 26, 29
Chinese Revolution, 79
Churchill, Winston
  1947 "Iron Curtain" speech, 110
Citizens Party, 82
civil rights laws, 61f
  assault on, 62
(*see also* voting rights)
civil rights movement, 74, 98
Civil War (1861-65), 9f, 52, 62
"class struggle from above," 98
Clinton, Bill, 78n, 100, 102
Clinton, Hillary, 105-109
cluster bombs, 4
Commoner, Barry, 82
Communist Manifesto, 21, 69
Communist Party USA, 53, 72-74, 75f
compulsory military service, 74
Congress of Industrial Organizations (CIO), 72
Constitution, US, 4-7
  2nd amendment, 25f
  13th amendment, 10, 49f
  14th amendment, 10
  15th amendment, 10, 52
  federal structure, 6f, 9
corporations, 10
counterrevolution, global, 22, 31, 73, 110f
court system, 13
Cuba
  in United Nations, 4
  war for independence, 30
  revolution, US opposition to, 41, 100
cultural transformation, 75f
culture (mass), 16-18

of celebrity, glamor,
violence, 12
of commercialism, 17
of conformity, 71
of conquest, 27
of cruelty, 16f, 67
of guns, 25, 61
of militarism, 23
of racism, 48, 52

Debs, Eugene V., 70-72
Declaration of
Independence, 5f, 30
deindustrialization, 63, 77
democracy
"excess of" (in 1960s), 15, 77
feared by Founding
Fathers, 6
as official ideology, 32
popular struggles, 3
Democratic Party (DP), 2f, 11, 78
blaming its 2000 defeat on Nader, 103
1944 choice of
Roosevelt's VP, 96
Democratic Leadership
Council, 78n
in recent elections, 81-86, 102-111
"super-delegates," 107
Democratic Socialists of
America (DSA), 88

"diversity," 18
division of powers, 9
double standards
on democracy, 42
on foreign intervention, 33f
on terrorist acts, 44
on torture, 40
drones, 23
drug trade, 63
(*see also* War on Drugs)
Dulles, Allen, 59, 97
duopoly
(Democrat/Republican), 8, 11, 82, 110, 113

"eco-terrorism," 87, 101
elections
1980, 78
2000, 7, 84, 102-105
2004, 85f
2008, 105f
2016, 7, 85, 105-109
electoral politics, limitations of, 85f
environmental crisis, 4, 23, 45, 86, 93, 113
Espionage Act, 71
"exceptional" traits of US, 12f

Federal Bureau of
Investigation (FBI), 59f

entrapment of Muslims, 100f
Federalist Papers, 6
financial crisis of 2008, 87f
flag, US, 24f
Florida
   in 2000 election, 103f
   2018 referendum on voting rights, 90
Food Stamps program, 97
Fox News
   role in 2000 election, 104
"free world," 14, 31
Freedom Schools, 54
"fusion" candidacies, 82f

Gay rights, 80f, 107
Georgia
   voter suppression in, 102n
Germany (Nazi period), 26, 73, 96
gerrymandering, 9
Giroux, Henry A., 16
Gore, Al, 78n, 102-105
   failure to challenge 2000 outcome, 105
Green Party, 84f
Grenada, US invasion of, 100

Hampton, Fred
   assassination of, 56-60
   original Rainbow Coalition, 56, 82
Harris, Katherine, 103f
Hawaii, 29
Haywood, Bill, 70
healthcare, 2, 13, 92
Helms-Burton Act, 100
Heritage Foundation, 77
Hikmatyar, Gulbuddin, 35
human rights, 4, 66
Huntington, Samuel P., 15, 77

immigration, 1, 14, 107
   (*see also* refugees)
imperialism, 21-45, 107
   distinctive features of US, 24-32
   economic and psychological aspects of, 44f
   linked to racism, 47f
   mindset of US supporters of, 23f, 35
Indiana
   prisoner correspondence in, 67
Indians/Native Americans
   massacres of, 3, 24-26, 29, 71, 92
   prior settlement, 4, 6
Industrial Workers of the World (IWW), 70
Iran, 28, 33, 78, 110

Iraq
  1991 US attack, 43
  2003 US invasion, 18, 37, 43, 86, 106, 110
Islamic communities in US
  surveillance of, 100
Islamic countries, 22f
Islamists, 34f
  ISIS, 37
Israel, 4, 23, 26, 101

Jackson, George, 90
Jackson, Jesse, 82
Japan, 26
  atomic bombing of, 96
Jews
  Nazi massacres of, 26

Kennan, George F., 42n
Kennedy, John F.
  assassination of, 59, 97
Kennedy, Robert F.
  assassination of, 59
Kerry, John, 86
King, Martin Luther, Jr.
  as civil rights leader, 54-56
  assassination of, 59f
Kiriakou, John, 40
Kissinger, Henry A., 41
Korea, 22, 100
Ku Klux Klan, 25, 50, 71

La Raza, 75
labor movement, 2f, 69f, 87
  industrial unionism, 72
  organizing in the segregated South, 53
  pro-capitalist leadership, 2, 61
  suppression of, under Reagan, 98
Labor Party, 83
landmines, 4
Latin America, 22, 29
lawyers, 13
League of Revolutionary Struggle, 79
"lesser evil," 81, 85
literacy, criminalization of, 49
lynching, 52, 61, 62, 95

Malcolm X, 55f
  assassination of, 55, 59f
Manning, Chelsea, 40
Marshall Plan, 110
Marx and Engels, 21, 69
Marxism-Leninism, 79
mass incarceration, 12, 14, 16, 61, 90
mass shootings, 12, 23f, 88, 91
McCarthyism, 74
media, 17-19, 58, 71, 105, 107
  alternative, 18f
  interest in having campaign ads, 11

 targeting Russia, 33
Mexico, 24
military bases, 22, 31
military budget, 42
military intervention
 double standards, 40
 ideology justifying, 35
 occupying foreign countries, 29
 political usefulness for US leaders, 37
 in Russia 1918, 22
money in politics, 11f
 (*see also* Political Action Committees)
Monroe Doctrine, 29
Montgomery bus-boycott, 54

Nader, Ralph, 84, 102-105
National Guard, 98
"national security," 60
New Communist Movement, 79f
New Deal, 73, 94f
 Works Progress Administration (WPA), 94
New Left (1960s), 74-77
New Party, 83
New York (state), 83
New York Times, 18
Nicaragua, 41f
Nixon, Richard M., 15, 41, 60f, 85

nonviolence, strategic, 55, 87
North Carolina
 voter suppression in, 109
nuclear weapons, 26-29

Obama, Barack, 37, 63,102, 105f, 111
obesity, 12n
"Occupy Wall Street," 88
Open Door policy, 29
Our Revolution (OR), 109-111

Pakistan, 43n
Palast, Greg
 on 2000 election, 103n
Palestinians, 4, 101
Panama, invasion of, 43, 100
Pennsylvania
 prisoner correspondence in, 67
permanent war, 93
Philippines
 US conquest of, 29
Physicians for a National Health Program, 80
police/policing, 16, 56, 62, 64f
 attacks on demonstrators, 54
 black officers, 62
 killings by police, 88, 91
Political Action Committees (PACs), 106

poverty, 12f
presidency, office of, 5
presidential debates, 84
prison labor
   as continuation of slavery, 10, 50
   fighting forest fires, 50n
   movement against prison slavery, 90
prisons, 64-68
   abuse of prisoners, 65f, 91f
   draconian sentences, 62, 63, 66
   solitary confinement, 66, 90
   video-visitation, 65, 67
Professional Air Traffic Controllers (PATCO), 98
Project for the New American Century, 43, 104
public schools, 7, 93
public services, 2, 94
   obstruction of, 13, 15
Puerto Rico, 30

"racial" division / racism, 1, 14, 107
   and imperialism, 47
   social definition of "race," 49f
   as weakening the working class, 1, 92
   (*see also* Ku Klux Klan, segregation)
Radical Reconstruction, 52
Rainbow Coalition, 56, 82
Reagan, Ronald, 15, 63, 78, 98
refugees, 23, 68, 92
"regime change," 48, 105
religion, 7, 13, 23, 71, 107
repression, political, 73f, 81, 97, 100f
Republican Party, 11, 78
   in recent elections, 102-108
   theft of 2000 election, 103f
"right to work" laws, 3
"rogue state," 34
Roosevelt, Franklin D., 73, 94, 96
ruling class, 48, 51, 61, 87, 111, 113
   claim to world leadership, 32
   contempt for accountability, 105
   invocation of democracy, 3
   current lack of restraint, 91-93
   need for climate of fear, 100
Russia

alleged role in US 2016 election, 33
US intervention in 1918, 22
US intervention in 1996, 33
(*see also* Soviet Union)

Sanders, Bernie, 105-111
DP steps to block his nomination, 107
founding of Our Revolution (OR), 109
views on foreign policy, 110
Saudi Arabia, 23, 26, 32, 34, 44n
Science for the People, 80
"security" (international), 31
segregation (Jim Crow), 52f, 62, 95
Selma-to-Montgomery march, 54
Serbia, bombing of, 100
sexual assault, 23, 88
slavery, 1, 6, 7, 9f, 14, 49-51, 92
incomplete abolition of, 50f
Social Security Act
race-related exclusions, 95
socialism, 69
popularity of, 88

Socialist Party of America, 70-72
Soviet Union
alleged military threat, 42f
collapse, 42, 79
and CPUSA, 72f
support of secular Afghan regime, 34
Truman support for Nazi attack on, 96
(*see also* Russia)
Spain, 30
Stein, Jill, 85
Stone, I.F., 36
Student Nonviolent Coordinating Committee (SNCC), 55f
Students for a Democratic Society (SDS), 75, 79
Supreme Court
1886 ruling on corporations as "persons," 10
2010 ruling on money in politics, 10
2013 overturning of Voting Rights Act, 9, 64

Talbot, David
The Devil's Chessboard, 59
terror, reign of, in the US South, 52
(*see also* lynching)
"terrorism," 32, 42, 87

terrorist attacks
  9/11, 43f, 87
  fear of, 48
torture, 40, 66
Trans Pacific Partnership, 106
Truman, Harry S., 96f
Truman Doctrine, 31
Trump, Donald, 13f, 17, 63, 88
  in 2016 election, 107-109

unionism, "business" vs. "social-movement," 2
United Auto Workers, 79
United Nations, 4, 66
USA Patriot Act, 87, 100

Venezuela, 42
Vietnam, 14, 22, 30
  resistance in US to war, 74
  US rationale for intervention, 36
vigilantes, 25, 55, 71
Virginia
  prisoner visits and correspondence, 67
voting rights, 7-9
  1965 Act, 9, 61, 64, 97, 111
  disenfranchisement, 8, 16, 64
  early 20th-century restrictions, 81
  limits on impact of elections, 51
  methods of voter suppression, 101f
  voter suppression in 2016 election, 108f

Wallace, Henry A., 96
war, as chronic US practice, 22f
war of independence (1775-83), 24, 29
War on Drugs, 15, 60-64, 77, 98
  prison sentences, 15, 63f
War on Terror, 42, 44, 100
Weather Underground, 79
welfare, 15, 63, 78
"Western values," 32
white supremacy, doctrine of, 48, 53
"white backlash," 63
Wisconsin
  impact of voter ID law, 108
women
  in Afghanistan, 35
  demonstration against Trump, 88
  healthcare funds for, cut, 92
  rights of, 4, 107

Women's Studies programs, 80
working class, 1-3
 absence of working-class party in US, 10
 class interest transcending "race," 48
 divided by race, 1
 greater influence outside the US, 28
 (*see also* labor movement)
world leadership, 32

World Trade Organization, 86
World War I, 71
World War II
 and economic recovery, 95
 segregated military units, 53

Yeltsin, Boris, 33
Young Lords, 75

Victor Wallis has been teaching in the Liberal Arts department at the Berklee College of Music (in Boston) since 1996, having previously taught political science for many years at Indiana University-Purdue University at Indianapolis. He was for twenty years managing editor of the journal *Socialism and Democracy*. He is the author of *Red-Green Revolution: The Politics and Technology of Ecosocialism* (2018). His articles – encompassing an array of subjects including ecology, political strategies, the US Left, US labor songs, current US politics, and Latin American revolutionary film – have appeared in *Monthly Review*, *Capitalism Nature Socialism*, *New Political Science*, *Socialism and Democracy*, *Jump Cut*, *Organization & Environment*, *International Critical Thought*, and the *Historical-Critical Dictionary of Marxism*, plus book-chapters and online publications in several countries, and have been translated into thirteen languages. He has lectured in Argentina, Brazil, China, France, Germany, and Peru. He was a Fulbright student in Chile in 1966-67. He directed the Indiana/California Program in Peru in 1982-83 and an International Honors Program semester in Europe in 1987. He was a Visiting Scholar at the Institute for Policy Studies in 1988, and a frequent commentator during the 1980s on Latin American issues and more recently on the ecological crisis. http://victorwallis.com

Johanna Fernández teaches 20th Century US history and the history of social movements at Baruch College (CUNY). Her book on the Young Lords, the Puerto Rican counterpart to the Black Panther Party, will be published in 2019 by University of North Carolina Press. In 2015, she directed and co-curated *¡Presente! The Young Lords in New York* an exhibition in three NYC museums cited by the *New York Times* as one of the year's *Top 10, Best In Art*. She is the editor of *Writing on the Wall: Selected Prison Writings of Mumia Abu-Jamal* (2015). With Mumia Abu-Jamal she co-edited *The Roots of Mass Incarceration: Locking Up Black Dissidents and Punishing the Poor*, a special issue of *Socialism and Democracy* (2014). Her awards include the Fulbright Scholars grant to the Middle East and North Africa and a National Endowment for the Humanities Fellowship of the Scholars-in-Residence program at the Schomburg Center for Research in Black Culture. She wrote and produced *Justice on Trial: The Case of Mumia Abu-Jamal* (BigNoise Films, 2010). Her mainstream writings have been published internationally, from *Al Jazeera* to the *Huffington Post*. She has appeared in a diverse range of print, radio, online and televised media including National Public Radio, *The New York Times, The Wall Street Journal,* and *Democracy Now!*

Kevin "Rashid" Johnson is a social prisoner who became politicized while incarcerated. As a result he became active in opposing and publicizing the abuses of US prisons. He also became an accomplished political artist and co-founded the New Afrikan Black Panther Party – Prison Chapter. In return prison officials have transferred him from state prison system to state prison system. Since 2012 he has been "compacted" from Virginia to Oregon to Texas to Florida; then back to Virginia and most recently to Indiana. These retaliatory transfers, which have seen him repeatedly held in solitary confinement, have not deterred his resolve. He is the author of *Defying the Tomb* (2010) and *Panther Vision* (2015). http://rashidmod.com/